A TEEN'S VOICE

LISTEN!

Teenagers: their challenging stories and how to **help** them

Ciarán McBreen

Breakfree Forever Publishing

Disclaimer

Author: Ciarán McBreen Title: LISTEN - Teenagers: their challenging stories and how to help them

ISBN: 978-1-9163736-4-8

Category: Personal Development/Teen/Family
Publisher: Breakfree Forever Publishing

Dedication

This book is dedicated to all the students who participated in the creation of LISTEN!; it would not have been possible without you. Thank you for allowing me to tell your stories.

I would also like to dedicate this book to those 'silent students', students experiencing emotional pain, students without a voice and who don't get to express themselves and be who they want to be. Please speak out and BE YOU, BE THE BEST YOU!

Acknowledgements

The creation of this project would not be possible without the involvement, help and support of many people. I would like to thank the following for their input towards this book, and also for the value they have added to my own personal journey.

To my wife Kim, you have always backed me in whatever path I feel the need to explore. Thank you for putting your trust in me. I am very grateful for everything you have done to make LISTEN! happen.

To my parents, sister and brother, thank you for your continued support in everything I do. I am very grateful for all you have done to make me the person I am.

To my friends, I am blessed to have great people around me. Thank you for your contribution to my journey and adding value to my life.

To my teachers, lecturers and educational organisations, thank you for giving me a platform to learn. As someone who was not academically gifted at school, I appreciate the efforts that were made to support my development.

To all the students that I have taught, thank you for adding great energy to my working day. I have been lucky to teach some outstanding students and some 'interesting' characters over the years. Each student brings a different dynamic to the classroom, making the job exciting and unpredictable. Thank you for allowing me to teach you.

To the coaches and coaching companies who trained me, thank you for giving me the skills, credentials and confidence to serve others.

To my coaching clients, thank you for allowing me to support you during our coaching sessions. It can certainly be a rollercoaster of emotions, but it is always worth it.

To my publisher, Michelle Watson of Breakfree Forever Publishing, you connected to my passion for writing this book, you fully understood my dream. Thank you for making this dream visible to others.

Finally, to the designer, Stephany Rodriguez, and editors, Sarah Antoniou and Kieren Knapp, thank you for your patience with me on how I wanted things to look. As each story in LISTEN! is written through the voice of a teenager, it was certainly challenging to keep each story authentic to the specific individual, while maintaining suitable language and expression. This was without doubt the most difficult part of the project. I appreciate your creativity and distinct eye. Apologies for being so specific! You did a fantastic job.

Thank you,
I am grateful to you all.

Chapters

Introduction

After working in the education industry since 2006, I have engaged with students from a wide range of nationalities, cultures and personalities. Personalities that all have different learning styles, needs and interests. Some excel in academic settings, whilst others thrive in sports and the arts. This brought a passion for teaching and learning and making sure that ALL students receive the opportunity to flourish in an educational environment that is safe, fun, creative and valuable to their future prospects. An education that connects students' learning to their interests, their personality types and their ways of learning.

However, the research I conducted for LISTEN! painted a different, worrying picture. It showcases that not all students recall positive experiences from their education. In the short stories included, it is clear that there is a considerable gap in what the students in the research need and what they are experiencing.

Each chapter is split into two parts:

PART 1 is the story, wherein the student explains their predicament and their views associated with it. Here, you will gain an insight into their personal experience when exposed to a challenging situation. Each story is unique in its own way, where the authentic voice of the storyteller can be felt and perceived.

PART 2 is the response from the author. This includes *Points to consider*, which encourages the reader to have an open mind about what they just read; the *CMB Wellbeing Warrior's* response, which includes coaching skills to support the topic; *Enquiry Questions* to link the reader to the students' challenge; and finally, a *CMB Task* is presented to encourage the reader to apply their newfound skills in their own lives.

My passion for creating LISTEN! and to work in the education industry stems from my own challenges at school. I was not academic, I had difficulties accessing the curriculum and sometimes lacked confidence regarding social acceptance and body image. I was a 'lost student' through the secondary education system and found myself finishing with basic grades that offered limited opportunities.

Looking back, I fully accept I didn't work hard enough during my school days, and I take complete responsibility for the outcome. Too often, I found myself gazing out of the window at the factory workers across the road, longing to be anywhere but my graffiti-covered, rickety school desk and the hard wooden chair I was sitting on. There was simply no connection to what I was learning, no interest in the subject and no relativity towards my future aspirations. As I sat there, I was either daydreaming about a football match on TV later on that night, or visualising myself playing and scoring a last-minute winner. This was where my creativity was at its best! The reality was that paying attention to the teacher was last on my to-do list.

I had ample support from home, and I would say that I was a completely different person outside of school regarding my personality and confidence. Sport had a significant part to play in this: it brought me to life, it got the best out of me. Playing sports put me in my element.

I anticipated the weekends impatiently, which consisted of participating in sports myself or watching games with my father. This was my platform to shine, engage and be who I wanted to be. Sadly, Monday morning always came around too fast, and when I heard the loud engine noise of the school bus coming around the corner to pick me up, an anxious feeling inside me was awakened for another week of school. It was countdown time until next weekend, five days to go!

Like many students during my school days, and sadly even today, there are still a large number of 'lost' boys and girls who simply cannot grasp the curriculum that is placed in front of them day in and day out. For me, it became apparent that only the academically gifted students would prevail, those blessed with the intellect and memory skills to sit and pass an exam.

I asked myself if this is an appropriate method of assessment. In these situations, do students demonstrate a clear understanding of knowledge, or is it just a case of memorising the curriculum? Sceptics like myself would argue it is the latter, but if this is the case, why begrudge those who experienced success from this model? Some students have great memories, and to put it simply, I did not!

Fast forward to the summer of 2001. My school life was over. I was relieved. I had finally made it. It was time to get out of here!

It must be acknowledged that I had some great people by my side who supported me through the five years, and I am forever grateful for them. However, the reality was staring me right in the face. I opened the brown envelope containing my results, alongside my wonderful friend on the side of a country lane, on a sunny August afternoon. Unfortunately, as expected, there were not many As or Bs on the results certificate. I left school with very much below average grades, which suggested no more than a bleak future ahead of me.

Thankfully, a local college, Cavan Institute, accepted my application. It wasn't university, but it was certainly what a student like me needed. The course I attended was vocational in nature and involved a practical element. I was studying sport. My academic interest grew from here. I could now connect learning to my interests. I had a new hunger, a new motivation and commitment to learn. I found a fresh belief in myself and I immediately began to reap the rewards. Within months I had gone from embarrassing grades to grades I could be proud of. I was delighted and reassured that I now had a chance in life!

This sudden transformation got me thinking and reflecting on my intellectual ability at school. Was I so bad after all? Obtaining these positive grades proved to me that I <u>can</u> learn, I <u>can</u> engage and I <u>can</u> prove myself academically.

In addition to this transformation, the assessment style changed. Third level education assessment was geared towards those who don't sit exams well. This consisted of assignments and practical assessments, as opposed to an exam worth 100% of the final mark. This supported my motivation as I had more control over the overall outcome.

Evidently for me, it is clear that there needed to be a connection to what I was learning, an interest and belief that I could do it. I must also recognise that I have worked tremendously hard since leaving school from an academic perspective, albeit because the connection with what I was studying was present. So what needs to come first? The academic ability or the interest? Or maybe a bit of both? You will know what suits you best. We are all different, but I now know what works for me.

This connection with what I was learning was missing back when I was at school, not just for me, but for many who went to school back in 1990s Ireland. For example, if a student achieved poor grades, they were classified as 'academically weak'. If a student misbehaved, they were classified as a 'naughty student' (to put it nicely!). Today, there is a vast amount of help to support these so-called 'lost' students. With differentiated lessons delivered by outstanding, creative teachers, one-to-one help provided by teaching assistants and even medication to support behaviour, it can be argued that students today never had it so good, where they have at least an opportunity to learn in a way that suits their needs, to have their voices heard and their concerns addressed. Unfortunately, some would argue that this is not always the case.

LISTEN! demonstrates that life as a teenager is not so straightforward, even with an extensive amount of supportive strategies available. The book is unique, insofar as it provides a case study for each topic to address the challenges involved. Each topic was conscientiously selected as a result of the findings from the quantitative data that was established during the research for this book. Every story you read will unearth a range of challenging situations that students of the 21st century find themselves in. From bullying to body image and studying to parental absence, the idea is that you, the reader, can gain an insight, by walking in the footsteps of these amazing students who are expressing their stories. Here, you will acquire a sense of the pain and trauma that they have gone through during their school years. My hope is that you will connect, you will reflect on your own experiences and, through the *CMB Wellbeing Warrior* section, you will engage.

The *CMB Wellbeing Warrior* section is significant and the learning that can be applied by the approach used is key to the readers' own responses to their personal challenges. Due to the topic and your own experiences, you will resonate with some parts more than others. The book doesn't claim to have all the answers and to fix all problems, but it will give you the tools and ideas to overcome your own demons. LISTEN! will make you think and ask questions of yourself, about your own behaviour and choices around others.

The book's origin and research results:

The idea behind the creation of this book came from witnessing first hand an enormous amount of pain from the many boys and girls I have taught during my teaching career. From working in London and Dubai, I observed a vast amount of challenging situations and problems that teenagers today are expected to deal with. School isn't easy, and as you read through the stories you will see that life, in general, is not easy either. The expectations put upon teenagers is tremendous and if we only knew what was going on inside their heads, we would all want to do more to help. Many children want to talk and do speak out; sometimes however, they are not heard. LISTEN! is exactly what it says it is. It will give you an insight into what is happening inside the mind of a teenager. It is about giving them a voice and simply listening to them.

The schools I have worked in are all drastically different, from a school consisting of students from challenging social-economic backgrounds in London to dealing with those with significant status and wealth in Dubai. However, from observation, even though there were major differences between both communities, it was clear that the similarities were remarkable. There was an absence in their lives. Both sets of students simply needed people to be present, available and to be heard. They needed people to *listen* to them.

This book is not just for students, but also for anybody who has any involvement with teenagers or future teenagers. It will support you in reading between the lines, asking the right questions, and acknowledging and solving challenges before they develop into problems.

The research for LISTEN! involved obtaining quantitative analysis from hundreds of children from 38 countries in an attempt to collect a comprehensive sample of personality types, cultures, curriculums, academic expectations and general teenage lifestyles. From San

Francisco to Sydney, from Thailand to Tanzania, the research for this book was globally extensive.

A selection of respondents to the initial survey was chosen to be interviewed, to compile qualitative analysis for participants to express their identified challenges in greater detail. It also provided the students with an opportunity to contribute further to their stories and fully express the heartache associated with their topic.

Each story you read is based on real-life events. However, some stories are amalgamated and altered, as they share similar themes. In addition, the names in each story have been changed, in order to preserve the participants' confidentiality.

It must be noted that you may find some stories disturbing. However, it was essential to include as much detail as possible to demonstrate a true reflection of the pain and distress suffered from the storyteller.

Key findings from the quantitative analysis demonstrated that academic pressure was rated as the highest challenge associated with the participants. This involved exam worries, grades, understanding how to study and pressure to complete homework. Furthermore, it was also found that anxiety, body image and public speaking were stated as other common challenges associated with the teenagers involved. Each topic mentioned is addressed in greater detail via the students' personal stories.

I hope that reading LISTEN! will be an enlightening experience for you, and that you will feel connected to each chapter in some way. At various points throughout this book, you may experience negative feelings, such as pain, hurt, disappointment, loneliness and failure, but it is only through traversing these difficult emotions that we can find the positives, such as joy, redemption and success. My hope is that, as you read through these stories, you will learn to express yourself with confidence, to encourage others to speak and to really *listen* to what they have to say.

I took great pleasure in writing this book. However, the pain and intensity of emotion in each story was significantly present, so prepare yourself for your own moving journey during this read.

Now, find a quiet and comfortable place to read, shut off the distractions of the outside world and open yourself up to these fantastic and wonderful teenagers who are kindly sharing their own story with you. *Listen* to what they have to say, *listen* to your own emotions during each story and *listen* to what actions could be taken in helping you become a better YOU!

1

Tanya: A Toxic Relationship

Hi there, it's Tanya here and I am 15 years old. Friendships, what are they all about? My experience with friends is complicated. It's like an interesting cocktail of different personalities. Some are nice and some not so nice. Like everyone, I try to select friendly people to be my friends. Just like going into a shoe shop: try on a pair, and if I like them, I keep them, and if not, I say, "No thanks!"

Is this attitude harsh? You will probably say it is, and you will probably be glad when you hear what happened next. Well, to keep things simple, I got a taste of my own medicine. I was the one being spat out and not wanted. Rejection, wow, this was all new to me.

One Monday after school, I received a voice message from my friend, Amy. It was a different type of message than usual. Amy is ordinarily bubbly and cheerful in nature. She usually starts a conversation with, "Hey BFF!" in a unique 'squeaky' sound of a voice. Yes, I accept that we are a bit cringy! But this was us, our weird and wonderful sense of humour and our understanding towards each other.

This message was different; this time, it was a serious tone of voice. It was not like her, and immediately I could sense that something just wasn't right.

"Tanya, I don't want to be friends with you anymore," she said.

"What?" I responded with a sense of confusion.

What did I just hear? I was dumped as a friend: OVER A VOICE MESSAGE! Wow, this hurt, and to make it worse, another friend who was with her, Sofia, shouted, "Yes, me too, I don't want to be friends anymore either." The message ended abruptly.

What just happened? Was this some sort of sick joke? I don't have loads of friends, and you're telling me that my closest friends are dumping me? But...no, this simply cannot be happening. We are a team, together forever we said. Everyone knows that! We just can't split up; we tell each other everything!

EVERYTHING!!

Then my heart begins to sink as I realise something: Amy knows things about me, things that even my parents don't know. This is a problem.

A rush of blood to the head. An excruciating pain in my chest. Panic sets in. Will she tell my secrets? The boys I like? The things I have said about other people? She knows too much. Who do I talk to now? Will she turn people against me? Ouch, my chest is pounding, this pain in my heart, I am struggling to breathe. I'm pulling my hair, my forehead is sweating. Loads of things are going on in my head. I'm all over the place, like I've lost control. I'm panicking; is this what a panic attack feels like?

Twenty minutes later, I'm lying on my bed, looking up at the ceiling. I can still hear the aeroplanes flying over my house when I reflect on this time. I am empty, lost and embarrassed. Why? What have I done to deserve this? I go on social media; I see pictures of the two girls together. I have been frozen out, ghosted! I'm dying inside; please tell me this is not happening.

I feel nervous going into school the next day, after a sleepless night. Part of me is angry, and the other part is hoping that it was all a big joke. In the corridor I see Amy and Sofia together on the way to my English lesson. My heart is racing; no, actually it's galloping as they approach me. Inside, I'm hoping that they'll laugh and hug me and say it was all a prank. But no, they blank me, they completely blank me. They walk by me as if I'm invisible. I feel devastated, abandoned, alone.

I sit down in class, but cannot focus. The pain won't go away. I keep fidgeting, sweating and, bizarrely, scratching my head. I tell the teacher that I feel sick and she sends me to the nurse. I pretend that I have a headache and have been vomiting. Yes, it's a lie, but it's how I feel inside, and so I'm sent home.

On the bus ride home, I sit by myself and rest my face against the freezing window. Warm tears are flowing down my face, a surprisingly pleasing feeling on my cold cheeks. What should I do now?

The whole week is brutal. I have nobody to talk to at school. I eat lunch on my own in a secluded part of the school, hidden away out of embarrassment. I mean, what can I say if people ask where the other girls are? I even go to the library to read after I finish my lunch, that's how bad it is! I feel mortified. I really do. Nobody wants me.

Nine days have passed (not that I'm counting), so perhaps it's time to accept the situation and make new friends. But where do I start? How do I pick them? Who do I like? Who likes me? Who is in the cool group? Ah, Jessica, everybody likes Jessica.

I approach her and say, "Hi Jess, how are you?"

"Hi Tanya," she responds.

We chit-chat for a bit, and I eventually ask if I can hang out with her and her friends at lunchtime. To my surprise, she says yes.

During lunch, we are all out the back of the school, talking openly about things I'm not used to, such as drinking and which guys we fancy, you know, stuff I used to think was private, just between besties! I am uncomfortable; it's not my scene. Some girls are smoking; ugh, I despise this so much! I get offered one and immediately see Jessica looking to see what my reaction is. What should I do? I don't know how to smoke. *I could really embarrass myself here*, I think to myself. However, if I don't join in, they may not like me. Remember, I need to be accepted into this new group. Do I give in to peer pressure, or do I stay strong and walk away?

I join in. I mean, what choice do I have? I have no friends, and this is a way of getting some, right? I shamefully do what they are doing. What would my parents say? They would not be happy. This is not me, is it?

After a few weeks, I notice I'm just like them, doing what they are doing, speaking like them and even looking like them. I have dyed my hair pink and I'm wearing dark clothes. I'm blasting music in my bedroom that I don't even like. Instead of doing my homework, I'm looking up song lyrics, learning the words to sing with my new 'friends'. Pathetic or what!

I want my parents to notice, but no, they are too busy doing their own thing, and even if they do notice they don't care; they simply don't *listen* to me when I need to talk. They are never at home. It's strange as they don't have jobs, so I don't know where they spend their days. Well, I do actually, but I'm too embarrassed to tell you. Let's just say they come home in a state that's not 'perfect parenting'! I have nobody to express my feelings to. I'm lonely, and it seems I'm losing my identity.

My attitude towards school has changed too. There is no engagement in lessons as this just 'isn't cool' in front of my new friends, and as for homework, well, as I said, learning songs took priority. My grades are dropping. Frighteningly, I simply don't care. Don't get me wrong, I'm outwardly happy, as I now have many friends, but in reality, inside, I am still lost. They are not really my friends. I don't talk to them about me, about my feelings. They don't know who I really am and I don't know them either. Oh, how I wish I could go back to my old friends. I miss them. I miss them so much.

> I want my parents to notice, but no, they are too busy doing their own thing, and even if they do notice they don't care; they simply don't *listen* to me when I need to talk.

One day after school, I see Amy and Sofia at the bus stop. I'm with Jess and the cool girls. I'm feeling confident; I have my new army by my side!

"Hey Amy," I say in a cheeky, sarcastic way. "Are you still too good for me, you b***h?"

Amy says nothing. I look at Jess. She pushes me forward, as if to say, 'keep going, give it to her'. I keep going, and continue to hurl abuse at my former friend.

Eventually, Amy responds: "Look, you and I just drifted apart. We're different people now. We have different interests, and it's time to move on."

Wow, now she has hit a nerve. Was this an answer to my question or a lecture? Different, DIFFERENT, she says. *For crying out loud, I'm only being different to fit in with people who I don't really like,* I think to myself.

I'm now furious, really furious. Does she 'actually' believe that she is too good for me? I'm not accepting this.

My new 'friends' egg me on. "Don't stand for that," Jess says, as she aggressively pushes me forward again. Things get heated. Ella, one of the girls from the group, steps in to have a go too. Now Ella is, well, let's just say large and mouthy, a brash character who can never resist a fight. Even the boys at school are intimidated by her! She is in her element here.

Ella goes up to Amy and pushes her. Amy is startled. Then, to my astonishment, Ella slaps her and pulls her hair, before throwing her against the bus stop window. It smashes. Amy is left lying in a pile of glass on the floor. Although I don't like this, I have to show allegiance to the girls. I then stand over her, spit on her and say, "Serves you right!"

Do I really mean this? No, of course I don't. Inside I am feeling very different. This is not me. I am not like this. Amy has been my best friend since primary school, since we were five years old! We have done everything together; she is like a sister to me. And yet here we are, on a wet and freezing evening in November, me standing over her as my new 'friends' nudge me on. Do I pick her up and apologise, or do I kick her while she is down? Where does my loyalty lie? I look around for some persuasion. The girls are looking at me, waiting for me to act.

I kick Amy. I kick her hard in the stomach. I have never done this to anybody before. Amy is in tears, clutching her stomach in pain and screaming on the floor. The rain bashes down on her and she is soaking wet. But she deserves this, right? Who does she think she is treating me like this? I showed her, didn't I?

As I walk away from the scene with my new entourage before the police arrive, I ask myself…Tanya, who have you turned into?

Points to consider:

- What do you think Tanya is really feeling here?

- Is her behaviour a reaction to rejection?

- Can you identify any benefits to what Tanya did at the end of this story?

- What consequences might she have faced if she had chosen not to do what she did?

- What would have been an ideal outcome here?

- Can you think of any problems associated with how Tanya is currently behaving?

What does the CMB Wellbeing Warrior say?

Tanya has experienced rejection, which isn't easy to accept. Rejection is painful to deal with, and let's be honest, none of us like to be rejected, no matter how big or small the situation. As soon as we are rejected, we immediately go into defensive mode and unleash the 'survival' part of our personalities. In this instance, Tanya's defensive mode was to hurt. Tanya is now on the attack!

When coaching Tanya, it is important to consider what she is feeling. Of course, it's easy to say that what she did was wrong. Physically harming anybody is wrong. However, as Tanya's coach, this would not be appropriate or helpful in moving forwards.

I would begin by asking Tanya to explain her behaviour and then justify it. Now, when I say justify, I mean it in a non-judgemental way, where she can openly express her reasoning behind such behaviour without me questioning it. This is key to a successful coaching relationship, as I am here to support Tanya, not discipline her. It is vital that she knows this, or else she may not fully engage.

By asking Tanya to justify what she did, I allow her the opportunity to demonstrate what she truly feels, from her perspective. Getting into Tanya's true feelings is the objective, as it will then allow us to eventually break away from this particular feeling and explore options for changing her behaviour.

To get a clear idea of what Tanya is feeling, we need to get to the truth. What we hear is not always an accurate account of what somebody is saying. In a session like this, I would use a skill I refer to as 'Co-listening'. Co-listening is when we read between the lines of what somebody is expressing. I would observe Tanya's body language, tonality and facial expressions to gain a deeper understanding of how she is feeling.

This can be learned in the *CMB Compelling Attentive Approach*. It goes beyond the words of what somebody is trying to convey, and with it, we can identify the true meaning behind their communication. In this example, it is me, the coach, who is using the Co-listening skills. However, by completing the activity, Tanya, 'the client', will also learn the acquired skills, which will make her a better listener. Obtaining such skills can improve our listening, as it provides us with the means to better understand the thoughts and feelings of individuals. This puts us in a better position to help them.

Have you ever expressed something when, in reality, you are feeling the complete opposite? We all have. The most common expression I have experienced from students is the phrase 'I'm fine,' even if their current situation is far from fine. When coaching, an excellent probing statement/question here would be:

"I can sense that you are saying one thing, but your body language and energy is telling me something different, so is there anything else I need to know?"

This allows the client to dig a little deeper and realise that they can't hide behind their words, and unless they open up, they are preventing themselves from developing.

Through Co-listening, we may find out that Tanya supports what she did. If this is the case, it's OK. Tanya is the client here, not Amy. It's essential to keep the focus on Tanya and not the issue of the fight. As coaches, even if we feel that her actions were wrong, we need to detach our own emotions, feelings and opinions and create a 'non-judgemental' environment, one where Tanya feels at ease to express what she needs to. Once we understand what Tanya is feeling and what Tanya wants, we can then proceed to the next stage of the coaching journey.

Enquiry Questions:

If you found yourself in a similar situation to Tanya, what would you have done? What would be the consequences of your actions?

CMB Task:

Task 1: Have you ever done something that you didn't want to do, but did it to impress others? Identify what it is. Write it down. Justify why you did it, but don't judge yourself. You may think differently now, but think back to who you were when you performed this act. Look at why it happened; there must have been a reason.

Now, explore a different option you could have taken back then. Think about what the outcome would have been if you had taken this different approach. Write down the answer and keep it in a safe place, as exploring this approach may serve you in the future. Hindsight is a great tool!

Task 2: Listen! Who in your life needs you to listen more? The next time you are in a conversation, try to be aware of your listening skills and be fully present with the other person. Bring your 'Co-listening' skills out in force.

2

Billy: The Jealous Bully

Hi there. My name is Billy. I'm good at sports and girls tend to like me, so I suppose that means I'm happy, right? Wrong! My sporting ability and appearance seem to give other boys a reason to give me a hard time. Jealousy is a big issue for me at school, particularly with one person called Jamie. Have you heard of the word 'anxiety'? It never leaves me!

I have always been pleasant and polite to people, boys and girls. I am lucky to be good at sports and most things I do. I suppose you could say I'm a talented individual; I like the sound of that! Every year on school sports day, I win many events. This gets me a lot of attention. Attention can be nice, but not all the time. It seems to have its consequences, unfortunately!

From the outside, you could say I am popular, always smiling and full of life. However, this is not a true reflection of how I feel on the inside. Internally I'm screaming, feeling hopeless, wishing I could confide in someone. I'm like a tiger in a zoo, looking good to the visitors but deep down feeling strained, restricted and simply lost. I just wish somebody would ask me how I feel. Have you ever wanted this?

The reality is that I'm not happy. Too often other boys are horrible to me. One boy in particular continues to give me a hard time: Jamie. Jamie has made many days at school difficult. I never got to know why really, but it was not a nice experience. In fact, it was horrendous. Here is my story.

One day during our PE lesson we were doing the high jump. Now, picture an old-style PE hall, wooden floor and gymnastic bars on the wall. Well, I think that's what they were, we actually never used them!

I was competing against the other boys in my class for the high jump. Thankfully I won and I beat the school record. This was a big deal. I am always a gracious winner and never get ahead of myself, it's not in my nature. Remarkably however, people tend to assume that because I am talented I must have a massive ego, a 'cockiness' of some sort. No, that's not me, that's not how I present myself; my dad wouldn't have it!

As I had broken the school record this particular day, the teacher asked me to keep jumping. So I kept jumping and jumping and the bar went higher and higher. I was in top form, jumping well and feeling invincible. This was my Olympics, me in my element, me in my happiness, at my best.

Lunchtime came and I was still jumping over the bar. The whole school could see the PE hall from the cafeteria, so they could see me jumping. Everyone cheered when I cleared the bar. They were even clapping for my take off, you know, the same way they do it on TV. This was awesome, I was feeling great, triumphant. I was enjoying this.

However, I soon came falling back to earth as I got a stark reminder of the pitfalls associated with being 'good'! As I was planning my run-up approach to the bar, I stood at the back of the hall. Here, other people were watching from the stairs of the balcony right above me. Right there, I felt a strange sensation on the back of my neck. I looked behind and saw Jamie. I felt my neck again and realised what had happened. He spat on me, his phlegm was slowly running down my whole back. It was disgusting. I just looked at him, empty, confused and simply thinking...why? And then the usual response from my body when I see Jamie. My anxiety levels increase. Heartbeat pumping, sweaty hands and overthinking: the monster is awakened.

He was intimidating and much more aggressive than me. He always tried to cause a stir, arranging to fight me in the field outside the school. I never wanted to fight, it's not me. Time after time I would run away from the scene. But how long could I keep this up?

Back to the high jump. I was standing there. Many people were looking at me with great excitement and anticipation. A wonderful moment in my school experience and I was smiling and feeling incredible. Well, that was what everybody else could see. How do you think I was feeling with Jamie's wet phlegm on my back?

What could I do? Jump? Run away? I actually wanted to cry, to be perfectly honest. I approached the bar and jumped in the air, raised my arms and pushed off the floor. Disappointingly, I hit the bar and landed on the mat. I had lost my rhythm, my mojo was gone. I was rattled. I had failed.

This is what bullies do, they make us lose belief in ourselves. As I hit the mat, all I could think about was Jamie's saliva that was now all over my back. Everybody clapped for me for doing so well, and I smiled and waved at them to say thanks. I looked happy and fulfilled, and why not? I had just broken the school record! This should be a memorable occasion, a moment that would live with me forever. Well, it hasn't left my memory, but unfortunately for the wrong reasons.

I went to the changing rooms and instead of feeling triumphant that so many people were cheering for me, I was in tears with disgust with what had happened. I felt dirty and sticky. Jamie had ruined my moment.

I sat there crying with my head in my hands. I felt confused and disgusting, stained with Jamie's slobber all over me. Why did he keep doing this to me? I had literally done nothing to annoy him, only be good at sports. Was this a crime? Surely not.

This wasn't the only time Jamie caused me problems. On another occasion, he walked by me in the school corridor. Punched me. He did this for no reason. Other people saw it and he laughed and got me in a headlock, saying that we were good friends playing around. Good friends, were we? There was actually a small part of me hoping that he meant this and that maybe all those years of torment were now over. No such luck; once the corridor was clear, his facial tone changed as he pinched my chest and twisted my skin. I was wrong, this wasn't over. He looked angry; something was not right with him. What was his problem?

This behaviour was a recurrence. One day we had a school trip. It was some sort of career fair. It was a local event, so we walked there, which was great. I loved getting out of school. I actually felt safer in 'the real world' than in school. It was a pleasant, fresh morning. Springtime and a warm day, so no coats on. We had to walk in single file, but everybody eventually mixed. I was happy here. I was at school but not really at school, if you know what I mean. Anyway, we got to the hotel where the event was. It was interesting, I was speaking to people from different companies. I liked this. In fact, this was giving me hope, hope for when I was out of this school life and away from Jamie. Ah yes, Jamie. Unfortunately, he was there. As I said earlier, he pounced on me on random occasions. It was not constant, thankfully, but sadly this was one of those occasions. Today was another day for Jamie, just when I was having a good day!

During the event, there was a performance. We were seated in chairs randomly. I was sitting next to Eva, a girl that I kind of knew, but would not talk to that much, as she was popular and very pretty. I was kinda shy on the inside, even if I projected confidence and assertiveness on the outside.

As we were waiting for the performance to start, Eva and I started talking. It was just a normal conversation, but we were getting on well and laughing away. Then, in the corner of my eye, I felt like I was being watched. I turned around; it was Jamie. The anxious feelings came immediately. His eyes narrowed. He looked like an anaconda ready to pounce!

I turned my head back, swallowed and thought: *Oh crap, something's up here.* Eva noticed something was wrong too. She turned around and saw Jamie.

"Ugh," she said, "he is so creepy! He asked me out last term, and I said no, but that wasn't enough for him. He follows me around, like a stalker! Oh, and he hates it when I talk to other boys. The last guy I chatted to, he actually beat up, can you believe it?"

"WHAT?" I gasped in a frightened tone. This was all I needed. "Thanks Eva," I muttered under my breath. My good fortune was helping me again. *Why did I have to sit here?* I thought to myself.

After the performance, I tried to keep my distance from Jamie. We all walked back to school and went to class. Then the bell rang for lunchtime. My heart was pounding, I didn't want lunchtime, I felt safer here with the teacher. Then the inevitable happened. Two boys came to tell me that Jamie wanted to fight me. Immediately, I felt the anxious pain in my chest again and the usual sweaty hands and nervousness that came with it. "Christ, c'mon give me a break here please," I groaned to myself. I told them that he had the wrong end of the stick, but they were having none of it.

I was lucky to have a good friend, a boy called Anthony. Anthony was able to manage himself in these situations. I was too, for that matter, but it was just not me, not my behaviour. I spent lunchtime playing badminton with Anthony, and I felt protected with him. Then along came Jamie and his mafia. "Billy, let's go," he said.

"Please leave me alone Jamie," I replied.

"You think you can flirt with my girlfriend and get away with it?" he asked. "She's not your girlfriend," I replied.

Jamie didn't like this. What had I done?

Then all hell broke out. He ran towards me. Anthony stepped in. Jamie's friends jumped in too. There were arms swinging everywhere. Bang! I was hit. I fell to the ground. A circle appeared around us: "FIGHT! FIGHT! FIGHT!" they chanted.

I tried to get up. There was a guy on top of me, a friend of Jamie's called Liam who was actually a nice person and someone I could chat with. Now he was fighting me, just to show his allegiance to Jamie. Was he brainwashed?

I turned him over, breathless and panting with fear. I felt afraid and totally out of my comfort zone. I was holding him. I couldn't do it, I couldn't punch him. It was not me. In the meantime, Anthony was wrestling with Jamie. It was all kicking off. Then…

FWEEEEEEEETT!

How glad I was to hear the teacher's whistle. Mr. Jackson to the rescue!

We had to explain ourselves in the principal's office, one by one and then as a group. I got in trouble, which is not like me, but it was worth it to hear Jamie say this all started because I was flirting with his 'fantasy girlfriend'. This made me chuckle. In fact everybody chuckled, even the principal, only for a split second, before covering it up with a cough. Jamie wasn't laughing though.

Time passed and attacks from Jamie continued on random occasions. The strange thing was that sometimes he would actually engage me in normal conversation, like a friend, and then other times give me grief. It was so unpredictable. I told my parents that this was happening over and over, but they didn't *listen*. They didn't see the pain I was in.

I couldn't take it anymore. I was having too many sleepless nights staring at the ceiling or sobbing into my pillow. I left the school in the end. Jamie had won, pushed me out. If only my parents took my claims seriously from the start, I wouldn't have had to go through so much emotional torture.

A few years later I bumped into Jamie in the toilets at a music event. I was now much bigger than him, and yet seeing him for the first time in ages stirred up those old feelings of anxiety, forcing me to recall all those awful memories.

> I told my parents that this was happening over and over, but they didn't *listen*.

What is he thinking? I wondered to myself. *What would he do?* Then, out of the blue, he turned to me and laughed.

"HEY BILLY!" he said. "Remember the fun times we had mucking about in Year 7?"

Silence in the room.

Fun times? I don't think so! I thought to myself.

"Fun? Really?" I responded, then smiled and walked away.

I felt good responding like that, filled with renewed confidence and self-worth. The whole experience, albeit very challenging, taught me many skills. Skills I knew would help me later in life.

A year or so later, I received a phone call. It was my friend Anthony. "Hey mate, this better be good as I'm winning on FIFA," I said.

"Hi Billy," Anthony says in a distinct and quiet low-toned voice. "I have some news for you. I'm not sure how you are going to feel about this, but…there has been an accident; Jamie is dead."

Silence…

…silence…

…and more silence.

I sat there looking out the window with a wealth of strange emotions. I genuinely didn't know what to feel. You know what, even to this day, I still don't know.

Points to consider:

- How do you think this experience would have affected Billy's academic development?

- Billy ended up leaving this particular school; what other options could he have explored during this difficult time?

- How did you feel about Billy changing schools?

- When Billy met Jamie at the music event, do you feel he handled himself well?

- Billy used the term 'control'; what do you think he is trying to express here?

- Billy sounds confused at the end of the story; why do you think this is the case?

- How would you feel after receiving that phone call?

What does the CMB Wellbeing Warrior say?

If Billy came to me as a client with this story, my main question would be: "What part of this do you want to explore?"

There is a lot going on here. Where do you think the focus lies, with the bullying or with Jamie's death?

Eventually, after some exploring and some powerful questioning, we would possibly unearth two different agendas. One could be his level of anxiety due to the bullying and the other is potentially his emotional feelings towards the death of Jamie.

From dealing with clients with similar stories, Billy may claim that the topic is bullying and Jamie's involvement in his life. In reality, the topic is not always the problem. We coach the person, not the problem. Here we would work on Billy and his responses to how Jamie has made him feel.

Expressing emotions can be challenging for many people. A useful tip if you do struggle to get them out is to write them down instead. In some cases, this can actually be a more powerful way to go about conveying how you feel, as more thought can go into it.

Articulating your feelings can develop how you perceive a particular situation. It's not easy, and in this instance I would validate Billy's honesty and reward his progress. In the coaching world, we call this 'championing'. This is a simple yet effective tool to use when we want to demonstrate acknowledgement towards somebody and the steps they have taken. Here is an example:

"Thank you Billy for voicing your feelings, it takes great courage to do this, well done."

You would be amazed at how reassured this makes clients feel early on in a coaching conversation.

It is important also to point out some key pieces of information we have heard from Billy. Billy has repeatedly mentioned his anxiety levels. 'Anxiety' is a strong word, sometimes overused and pervasive in modern culture. It is often conflated with 'worry', which is NOT the same feeling. Billy has experienced pain in his chest, sleepless nights and sweating. Physiological symptoms like these demonstrate clear signs of anxiety, whereas 'worry' can manifest as psychological symptoms. This is something that tends to be prevalent among teenagers today and needs to be given attention. In her book *'Press Play'*, about student wellbeing, Linda Bonnar wonderfully differentiates them both, check it out.

In this instance, it would be advisable for Billy to seek medical help, alongside his coaching sessions, as anxiety can have a major influence on an individual's performance in life. It must be treated very seriously.

Let's say that Billy decides that he wants to discuss his anxiety and the feelings associated with it. During the session, he expresses that every time he thinks of Jamie his anxiety appears, and he knows this, because of the physiological symptoms he is experiencing. When coaching, there is an unwritten rule, that we focus only on the present and the future. However, although Billy's memory is in the past, it is important not to disregard this, as it is still affecting him. Some flexibility to the 'coaching rulebook' is needed here. If the trigger is still present through memory, and if Billy needs to address it, then I have to appreciate this and be fully present for him. As a coach, sometimes we need to take control of the conversation, but at other times it is best to let the client lead the way. In this instance, Billy is delving into his past, albeit with a strategic purpose from the coach of moving forward.

As stated in this example, the agenda is Billy's anxious feelings. There are various methods that can be used to help people deal with their anxiety. Variety in the methodology is crucial, as some approaches may work well for one person, but have an adverse effect on another.

One activity that tends to be successful for many struggling with anxiety is 'deep breathing exercises'. These can be learned and then conducted alone in a client's own time when the anxious feelings appear. In a session, we do this through the *CMB Mindful Magic Matrix*. I have been amazed by how well clients respond to this method.

A typical session like this involves performing a series of different breathing and mindfulness activities. The objective here is to assist

Billy, to relieve the physiological pains associated with his anxiety. This could be accompanied by some visualisations that will help Billy detach his feelings from the trigger, which in this case manifested from his bullying experience.

A practice like this will go some way to support Billy in attempting to let go of the past and live in the present day. It will allow him to focus on what is in front of him today and beyond, without the presence of triggered anxiety. Through focusing on the present, he will hopefully realise that until he is ready to let go of the past, his anxiety will dictate his present and future life.

We could further explore how allowing these feelings to come to light is serving him at present and look at the effect it has on his life. A good question here would be: "What would life be like if you didn't allow these emotions to take control?"

Eventually, Billy will begin to see that these old experiences are in no way helping him move on and, until he brings them under control, they will continue to interfere with his life, even without the bully present.

Enquiry Questions:

If you were Anthony giving Billy the news about Jamie's death, and Billy responded with, "I don't care that Jamie is dead, he really hurt me and I don't forgive him," what would you think of Billy? What would be the best response?

CMB Task:

Task 1: Look around at the people in your life. Can you identify anybody who, on the outside, looks confident and happy? Do you really think they are? What can you do in order to see beneath their 'confident' outer shell?

Task 2: If you are ever feeling anxious or under pressure, have a go at doing your own deep breathing exercises. There are many approved methods which you can research. Through some exploration and practice you will discover what works best for you. Here is a short and simple one to start you off:

Step 1: Place yourself in a comfortable position.

Step 2: Breathe in through your nose for 10 seconds.

Step 3: Hold for 10 seconds.

Step 4: Exhale through your mouth for as long as you can.

Step 5: Repeat this 5 times.

3

Prisha: My 'Princess' Sister And My Controlling Friend

'm Prisha. I am OK with life. Well, it's sometimes boring, plus school can be a bit stressful at times, but other than that all is good. Don't get me wrong, I do have my challenges, like everyone else. I suppose nothing comes easy, well, at least that's what my dad always tells me. "You have to work hard for it, you get whatever you put in," he says in his deep Indian accent! Home life is fine. We live in a beautiful house in a nice part of town. We are financially stable, which gives us freedoms that we sometimes take for granted.

This all sounds perfect, right? It probably does, but I do have my problems. I can think of three major ones right now that affect how I feel in life. One is my sister, one is my friend and another is the pressure of school.

Let me start with my sister Saira. Do you know what her name means in Hindi? You're not going to believe it. It means 'princess'. Yes, behold the princess! I have never met a person more suited to a name than Saira. It's as if my parents knew how she would turn out!

I hate being measured up to Saira. It happens all the time. At home, I hear: "Why can't you be more like your sister?" At school, my teachers fawn all over Saira and say things like: "Your sister was good at this subject," and one teacher even followed this up with: "What happened to you?" Can you believe it?!

Like come on, how unfair is this? Some days I just want to stand up on my chair, throw the table to one side, grab my teacher by the throat and shout: "I AM NOT MY SISTER! I AM ME, PRISHA!" But no, I've never done it, not yet anyway!

So, who is Saira? Allow me to paint a picture for you. Imagine a version of me, but two years older, slimmer, prettier and just better in every way. Yes, Saira is your typical PERFECT girl, PERFECT daughter and PERFECT student. Long brown hair, tanned skin, long legs, good teeth, she has it all. Pocahontas, people call her. You get me now?! Me, not so perfect. I have bad teeth, I'm not what you might call slim and, let's face it, I am the 'ugly' sister.

To make it worse, Saira is not nice to me, not one bit. She calls me names and laughs at everything I do. She treats me like a child. She is dominant, so dominant. Everything that happens at home is done to suit her. Like for example whenever we discuss holidays, it's always Saira's decision. "Shall we go to this place?" mum would ask her, and she'd reply, "Nah, I wouldn't be seen dead there! Let's go here instead. I think my followers would like that better."

Ah yes, Saira's followers. It is all about image. Her Instagram is everything to her. She likes to think of herself as an influencer. I think it's pathetic really! Eventually, we just give up and say, "OK Saira, you tell us where you want to go."

She has a complete princess attitude, especially when it comes to boys. No boy in our school is good enough for her; 'apparently' they're too immature. If she's gonna date someone, it has to be a boy from another school or somebody older than her. I don't get it.

As for me, I get lost within our family. I don't get a say in anything. My parents don't *listen* to me, unless I mention Saira for whatever reason, and then they pay attention.

I know those of you who have experienced this will understand exactly what I am feeling; the constant comparisons to my perfect sibling; the daily reminders that I'm not as good as her, not as talented; I'm not Saira.

It's not nice. It's hurtful.

When we get introduced to people, they are shocked that we are sisters. It's like they look at me with disappointment. I can see it in their eyes, their whole face changes to a sense of pity or something like that. I have even wondered if we are biological sisters, honestly, it's that bad sometimes. And to make it worse, everyone thinks she is lovely. But she really isn't. She would talk to you and be all smiley and sweet, but as soon as you're gone, she'll make nasty comments about you, like, "Ugh, did you see his teeth?" or, "Ew, the state of their house."

> My parents don't *listen* to me, unless I mention Saira for whatever reason, and then they pay attention.

Saira might be Pocahontas on the outside, but on the inside, she's Veruca Salt from Charlie and the Chocolate Factory, a nasty, domineering, spoiled brat!

Another challenge I have is with my friend Neha. Neha is a control freak. When I'm with her, every decision I make is wrong, and of course she has the answer. It's like I don't have my own mind. And then, when I don't do what she wants me to do, she sulks. She even threatens me at times when I don't do what she says.

One day, I disagreed with her opinion about another person. I'll never forget the evil look she gave me, and also the horrible thing she said to me:

"Go on then, go find other friends, you are nothing without me."

I mean come on, do I not have a say in my own thinking? I find this controlling nature problematic and even scary at times.

Neha always has to outdo me. If I say that we went to a fancy restaurant, then she went to a better one. If I get a new smartphone, she immediately gets a new one too, even if the old one was not broken. She needs an upgrade on everything.

I just don't know what to do. Don't get me wrong, sometimes I like who she is and I enjoy her company. But then there's this 'controlling' nature inside of her towards me. It's just bizarre.

I'm sure people around us notice it. Even my teachers have pulled her up on it. Sometimes she signs me up for things without my permission, just so she's not on her own. For example, on sports day she put my name down to do the long jump with her.

"Long jump!" I gasped. C'mon, I have never done the long jump in my life. I don't even know what it is. Something to do with jumping for a long time I presume…

My teacher knows the situation and can see what is happening. She responds with: "Why don't we let Prisha decide for herself what she wants to compete in for sports day?" Then I get *that* look again. The vicious look. The look of terror from Neha. She doesn't say anything; she doesn't have to, because her eyes are screaming, *'You'd better do what I want you to do, or else.'*

Or else what? I think to myself, but then I eventually give in. I don't want the hassle, I don't want the trouble of falling out with her and stuff. I mean, what good would it do? Long jump it is!

She knows me too well, she knows things about me that nobody else does. If we 'break up' as friends, she may disclose my secrets to other people. Part of me is scared of what she is capable of when she behaves like this. It's not normal. I really think she has a problem.

My final challenge is school, or to be more specific, my school grades. I'm sick and tired of all the fuss. It's all around me, it really is. I cannot get away from it. At the breakfast table from my parents, all day at school from my teachers and then at the dinner table from my parents AGAIN!

"How are your grades on this subject?" "What did you do wrong there?" "You need to spend more time studying."

MORE TIME? Are you joking?! There is literally no more time! My life is taken up by studying, and my grades are always under scrutiny. If I get a C on a test, then why not a B? If I get a B, then why not an A? And of course, if I do somehow get an A, then the test must have been too easy! I just can't get away from it. I can't breathe, honestly, I can't!

I get tuition for most subjects and it's constant. The number of times my mum says, "Do you know how lucky you are to have this tuition?" OK, I get it. I am lucky, but as far as I am concerned, not as lucky as the people playing outside, getting to go for a walk in the park or simply sitting in their room, on social media or watching Netflix.

It's embarrassing really. I hear it all the time at school. "Oh, did you watch this or did you watch that?" For me, it's always a no. A big fat NO! I have to do school all over again, but this time at home. I mean, I have sat at a desk for eight hours all day at school and now

I have to do it at home too. And this is after my homework. School, homework, tuition. I'm suffocating, but nobody can see.

Listen to this for a daily routine. I get up, eat breakfast, freshen up and go to school. After school, I come home, eat a snack and change out of my uniform. I then do my homework and eat dinner. Then my Business Studies tutor arrives and sticks around for an hour, only to then be replaced by my Science tutor. And that's on the quieter days; some days four tutors will come. FOUR! Sometimes I'm being tutored way past my bedtime, and it doesn't stop when school stops: I'm studying on the weekends and even during holidays. How boring is that?

I have said it to my parents on many occasions that this will drain me, it will destroy me, it will kill me. But they don't listen! I'm an object, a robot, stuck in an endless, soul-crushing loop. I'm losing my hunger for learning; it's disappearing bit by bit, and I know that it will eventually be gone if I continue in this fashion. Gone, because I'm simply 'pushed' too much.

Can you imagine an Olympian training day after day and then turning up for the Olympics feeling fresh and ready to compete at their best? No, me neither, they will be physically burned out. Instead, they will have a programme, a balanced programme where they are involved in the designing process. They will have autonomy over their own decisions, free to choose the regimen that best suits them. 'Free to choose', wow, I wonder what that feels like. How I long for my parents to one day say, "Prisha, do YOU WANT to do this?" or, "Prisha, do YOU THINK this would benefit you?" Wow, imagine that; I may actually start to make progress!

I'm dreading the end of year exams. I'm not prepared for them; I'm burnt out. I need help, but nobody is listening to me, nobody. I want to scream at the top of my voice, "THIS IS NOT WORKING

FOR ME!" But I won't, it's pointless. I'm invisible. This is my future and I have no control over it. It really sucks!

So that's me, that's my life. I'm controlled at home by my sister, controlled at school by my so-called friend and I'm controlled 24/7 by the pressure on my school grades. I was wrong at the start; my life is not fine, it's clearly not.

Points to consider:

- Do you think that Prisha is right to feel the way she does about her sister?

- Could she take more control over how she feels?

- Regarding Prisha's academics, could she see this more as an opportunity as opposed to a burden?

- How did Prisha get herself into the situation with Neha? How might she resolve it?

- With regards to her parents, what do you think their agenda is?

- What is stopping Prisha from expressing herself to her parents?

What does the CMB Wellbeing Warrior say?

There is clearly a lot going on here and there are three likely topics that Prisha would like to discuss: her sister, her friend and her education. There is an agenda that underpins these issues however: 'control', something Prisha doesn't seem to have. Here, Prisha needs to examine what she has control over, and what she does not, and then manage the situations she finds herself in.

It is also evident from Prisha's story that there is a great deal of judgement present with regards to Saira, her sister. She is comparing herself to Saira and clearly, this is not serving her. When we compare ourselves to others, it can negatively affect our self-esteem.

From hearing Prisha's story, it sounds like there is a part of her behaving in a way that is not helpful. A hidden enemy within us, such as this, can hold us back from achieving our full potential. During a coaching session with Prisha, I would employ the *CMB Space Invader*. Essentially, your *'Space Invader'* is the part of your personality that is sabotaging your dreams, impeding your developments, that inner voice that tells you, *you're not good enough*.

We have many types of *'Space Invaders'* that need consideration in order for us to continue to move forwards with our personal development. In this instance, the *'Space Invader'* that is present is Prisha's *'Competitive Critic'*. A *'Competitive Critic'* surfaces when a person criticises themselves, when they measure their self-worth against the worth of others.

Prisha brings her *'Competitive Critic'* alive when she competes with Saira. She is pitting her own looks, intelligence and achievements against her sister's. This is having a negative impact on how she feels.

When conducting a session like this, Prisha would face her *'Competitive Critic'* and, by being curious and creative, will develop the skills to break it down, look at its behaviours and the effect it is having on her and attempt to take control of it. By understanding it more, we are empowering Prisha to weaken it, where it will have a lesser impact on how she feels.

The outcome here is that Prisha will be able to understand and manage her *'Competitive Critic'* whenever it turns up in the future. If Prisha allows her *'Competitive Critic'* to dominate her, then the outcomes will not change and she will continue to experience the same negative feelings. So instead, it is significant for Prisha to be 'in charge' of her *'Competitive Critic'*, in order for it to have a lesser influence on her feelings.

During this coaching activity, we kick our *'Competitive Critic'* off a proverbial cliff! This humorous yet effective visualisation differentiates the *'Competitive Critic'* from the person and has powerful consequences the next time it pops up unexpectedly. Take control of your *'Competitive Critic'* and give it the boot!

Enquiry Question:

Imagine if Prisha weakened her *'Competitive Critic'*. What do you think would change in her relationship with her sister Saira?

CMB Task:

Task 1: Take a look at yourself and your behaviours. When are you critical of yourself, and when do you compare yourself to others? How is this behaviour serving you? Are you punishing yourself for something that you cannot control? What if you can take back control?

Have a think and see what triggers your *'Competitive Critic'* and explore what is possible if you could take control over it. Be strong and weaken your *'Competitive Critic'*.

Task 2: Similar ideologies of different personalities within us sabotaging our behaviours can also be seen in a wonderful book, called *'Positive Intelligence'*, by Shirzad Chamine. Have a read and see what you can learn about your own behaviours!

4

Alfie: Academic Jealousy And Body Image Worries

Hello. My name is Alfie. I've always been enthusiastic about studying, from an early age. I could happily spend hours at my desk with an immense thirst for knowledge, running on nothing but the occasional cucumbers and grape juice. My favourite subjects are Maths and Physics, the 'nerdy' stuff.

Unfortunately however, this has caused me problems with the people in my classes. For example, one day in Biology, the teacher used the wrong term when we were learning the skeletal system. She said 'toe bones' when discussing the bones of the foot. I automatically corrected her and highlighted that the actual scientific term for them was 'phalanges'. Yes, I know it probably made me look presumptuous and a little disrespectful of the teacher, but hey, it's me! Everyone in the class suddenly turned in their seats to look at me with disgust or, as I like to tell myself, jealousy, as to how I knew this at my age. I mean, what's wrong with being knowledgeable? Is it not cool to be smart? Why does being good at sport or music make you popular, but knowing what phalanges are makes you weird? They are all talents, right? All worthy of praise? Well, going by what happened next, I really don't know at all!

That lunchtime I was in the canteen, eating by myself and minding my own business, when two boys came over to me. *Here we go*, I thought to myself.

"Hey geek!" one of them said. "You think you are better than the rest of us?"

I consider myself a strong-minded person and I let stuff like this go, as I'm well used to it at this stage. But then the other boy commented on my appearance. "The state of you anyway, look at you, skinny as hell," he said.

This came out of nowhere and had nothing to do with the conversation. He continued: "Why are you so skinny, do you not eat?"

I sat there in silence. I wanted to respond with: "But you are fat, it's not like you are perfect is it?" But I didn't; I sat perfectly still and took the abuse. They wanted a reaction out of me, but I was determined not to give it to them. In saying that, I don't have the guts to challenge people. I literally couldn't say to him that he was fat. One, because I didn't want to get into a fight and then get into trouble, and two, because, well you know, I actually didn't want to hurt his feelings. How stupid is that? He is right there in my face insulting me and I actually care about <u>his</u> feelings. Am I pathetic or what? What kind of behaviour is this? Where will this get me in life? Walked over? Going by this incident, then yes!

The funny thing is, most people actually seem to think that it is OK to call people skinny. I HATE this word. Please, never use it. Even in my family, my aunties call me skinny and say things such as, "BOY, why do you not eat?" But I really do eat. I eat surprisingly well, I eat healthily and I eat plenty, trust me I have done my research. I tell them this, but they just don't *listen* to me. This is who I am, it's my body makeup. Sometimes I just want to scream out loud, "I DO EAT, LEAVE ME ALONE!"

My body, my metabolism and my appetite is just different from others, that's all. Is this a problem? It's not a problem to me, but people make it a problem, and when enough people say it, it becomes my problem. It makes me paranoid. What are they thinking about me? Calling me skinny behind my back perhaps? I don't know, maybe I'm getting overly suspicious.

> I tell them this, but they just don't *listen* to me.

Ironically, thinking about my aunties, they are fat too, just like the guy at school. It is comical to me as to why it's OK to call somebody skinny but not OK to call somebody fat. Both are insulting, right? So why? I just don't get it at all.

Before I was fine with it. In fact, because I wasn't really thinking about it, it didn't bother me. But now...now with this paranoia and constant reminder in my head that *I AM SKINNY*, I see things that I didn't see before. For example, when I look in the mirror, I see my ribs, my skinny arms and my skinny legs. Oh, I really hate my legs!

I just cannot put weight on, even if I eat loads. I check out other boys' physiques and compare myself to them. I look at them and make statements to myself such as: "I wish I looked like that," "The school uniform doesn't look like that on me," and "Why do the PE shorts hang off me, but on other people they look good?" It's as if I'm punishing myself, asking questions that seemingly have no answers, hoping that somehow things will change.

It's lonely being me. I have no place in society. I'm mocked for the things I'm good at and mocked even harder for what I'm bad at. I'll admit that I'm not good at sports. Everyone laughs at me during PE, at my thin physique, my lack of skill and strength in games like football and rugby. I'm trying my best!

I get it, I don't belong here. I don't belong with these people. Where do I belong then? I don't know. I just wish I could meet people with similar interests to me. People who support my talent and don't laugh at my flaws.

For now, I am alone. Nobody at school gets me. I hate it. I hate school, I hate my body, and I hate that I have nobody to share my feelings with, nobody to have my back and nobody to embrace who I am. It's hurting, it's hurting real bad.

Points to consider:

- How can Alfie celebrate his academic achievements as opposed to feeling the way he currently does?

- What can he say to people who call him skinny?

- From a physical perspective, is there anything Alfie could do with his body in order to feel more comfortable in it?

- What resources could Alfie use to support his physical development?

- Can you identify how Alfie could meet people with similar interests?

- Alfie mentioned that he would get walked over by being a 'nice person', what do you think he means by this?

What does the CMB Wellbeing Warrior say?

It is clear to see that Alfie is not in a good place. There are two themes evident in this story: his strengths (intellect) and his weaknesses (sport and negative body image). Let's focus on the first theme: intellect. Yes, he is gifted academically, and this is something that he should be proud of, not embarrassed about. He could embrace this and shout out to everybody as loud as he can, "I AM ALFIE AND I AM GOOD AT THIS."

I am a firm believer that everybody is talented at something, be it in the world of sport, art or academia. We all have a 'strength' in us. Conversely, we cannot be good at everything, and those aspects we struggle with we call 'weaknesses'. Sometimes we focus so much on our weaknesses that we forget about our strengths. It is vital to appreciate the strengths you have, as this creates more positive energy for you. What do you think happens when you focus more on your weaknesses?

During a coaching session in this instance, through the *CMB Gratitude Growth Generator*, we explore any strengths Alfie has and identify what he appreciates about them. We break down the characteristics and skills involved and see how we can utilise these in other areas of his life where he may be experiencing some challenge. For example, let's look at one of Alfie's weaknesses: sport.

Alfie has said that he is not good at sport. This is fine; as stated, we cannot be good at everything, right? So instead of focusing on this weakness, we can utilise one of his strengths, in this case academia, and see if we can build an interest in sports. Here, we could focus on the mechanical movements of the body when playing football. We could talk about which muscles are used to kick a ball, or how best to avoid injuries. I'm not saying that this will make him better at the game, but it might give him more of an interest and therefore his approach to the subject or activity may change. By changing the approach, the outcome could be different.

Alfie may have to change the approach many times in order to get the desired outcome, but through this exploration, he is learning what works and what does not. Failure during this journey is expected and welcomed, and the learning that he can take from such failure is immeasurable to future developments. The key to dealing with failure is not to take it too seriously; accept it, don't be too hard on yourself, smile and move on!

Regarding Alfie's negative body image: this is a topic I have heard many times from clients. I have personally struggled with this myself, when I was a teenager, and even now as an adult at times the feelings emerge. Our bodies change rapidly throughout our adolescence, and it's common to feel awkward at this time of your life. The truth is that negative body image is something that can carry on well into adulthood. Not all people are comfortable in their own skin, even if you see them on social media posting pictures of themselves and 'showing off' their physiques. That 'perfect' influencer you follow, with their aesthetically pleasing physique and photogenic face, might be harbouring their own demons and insecurities. This is the part you don't see as you 'scroll', 'like' or 'comment'.

Sometimes, we all want to be something we are not, this is natural. What Alfie is doing here is comparing his body against others. This will not help his situation or his feelings. Everyone's body makeup is different and it reacts differently to diet and exercise. What works for them may not work for Alfie and vice versa. What is key here is that we examine what will work for Alfie. We need to look where he is now, and where he wants to go, and design an achievable target.

Again, using this self-appreciation approach, we can see how best to utilise Alfie's body issues to his benefit. For example, he may feel self-conscious about how skinny his legs are, but we can change that, we simply need to be resourceful. We want to reframe his thinking and encourage him to be flexible and open to different viewpoints.

The word 'skinny' carries negative connotations and can trigger negative feelings in Alfie. We need to first change his perspective on the word 'skinny' into something more helpful for him.

Once we can detach these negative feelings with the word, we can then explore other possibilities. I would ask Alfie questions like: "What is good about your legs?" or, "What is possible with legs like yours?" I would get him to explore this and ideas would arise. For example, he may find out that certain clothes compliment a slimmer physique such as his. He might discover that his muscles have great endurance. If this is the case, we would examine the possibility of him taking up some long-distance activity, such as running or cycling. Can you think of any more? Could you imagine what would happen if Alfie ended up being successful at running, cycling or dancing maybe? Yes, he would find a new appreciation for them, and his perspective would change, from 'hating them' to 'appreciating' and 'accepting' them.

It's important to remember that there are pros and cons to many things in life, even our bodies. We need to explore the options available to us until we get the desired outcome. The exploration alone can be a very rewarding journey and a great deal of learning will take place. We need to embrace what we have and what tools we have at our disposal.

You only have one body, your body, so try not to compare it to others. Maximise your body's resources and take full advantage of what is possible with it.

Enquiry Question:

If there was a person like Alfie in your life, what could you do in order to support how he or she feels?

CMB Task:

Look at your own body. How do you feel about it?

If you are feeling positive, great! If not, don't be too hard on yourself; most people are feeling exactly what you are feeling right now.

Make a list of the things you like about your body and the things you dislike. Regarding the parts you like, remind yourself daily how much you like them. Smile! Every time you think of the part you dislike, fight back with a reminder of the part you like. Embrace how lucky you are to be like this. Everyone will be different. It could be as simple as having an able body, or being aesthetically perfect (if there is such a thing!), everyone's is personal.

Now, what about the parts you dislike? Like Alfie, explore what you can do about this. If you want to change it, then look at what you have control over and do something about it. Alternatively, if you don't have the desire to do anything, then maybe it doesn't bother you as much as you think!

This part that you dislike, name it. Write down what has to be done in order for you to feel differently about it. List the stages and processes that need to take place for a change of feeling to happen. You would be surprised, as by simply 'thinking' about taking action, you actually begin to feel much better about it. You are now feeding your body positive energy!

Contrarily, you can control your mind into 'accepting' it by changing your perspective. This is a mental challenge between you and…you! It's your body, it's your choice, you always have a choice. Each choice has a consequence, so the big question is: can you deal with the consequences if you don't change your way of thinking?

You are in charge, so take charge!

5

Sarah: School, Knowing How To Study And Writing Exams

SCHOOL: Nope, not for me! I don't like school, but then again, does anybody? I suppose those who get decent grades and have good friends probably enjoy school, but not me. In fact, I don't conform to school life at all: I hate studying, I don't want to work in groups and I especially hate my teachers. They are so dull, with their uninspiring lesson plans and droning voices. They don't care about teaching; it's just a paycheck to them and a job with loads of holidays. Well, some of my teachers do things differently, but the rest of them are *bor-ing*!

The problem is simply this: I can't learn anything in this environment. In class I'm supposed to sit and listen to a teacher talk *at* me for hours, usually about stuff I don't care about. They talk *at* me, not *to* me. What's the point of going to school? I could just as easily set up a Zoom Meeting from my bedroom!

I'm sick of being told what to do, at home and in school. Everything is a routine, *get up at this time, go to school, learn this, learn that, go home, homework, dinner, bed.* So regimented! I need the freedom to make my own decisions, to make my own mistakes. I need my teachers to be open with me, to be fun and engaging. Yes, I like when the teacher is nice and pleasant to me. There is mutual respect and they treat me like a human being, not like a child. It's like, give me freedom and my talent shines, restrict me and nothing happens! Isn't this the best way to learn? I'm not alone in thinking this, right?

The thing is, I'm actually quite good at some subjects. I tend to get good grades in PE and DT. What does this tell you about me? It shows that I'm practical and creative, that I work well with my hands. I don't know what I'll do after school, but I reckon I'll be working outdoors. No desk job for me! But what about my other subjects? A waste of time as far as I'm concerned. Like, take Maths for example: what's the point of it? We have calculators now!

I think that the current education system is so outdated. It needs to be torn up and rewritten as something new and fresh, something that will better prepare us for modern life.

This is what I think anyway. Is this mindset restricting me? Does it impact my commitment to learning? Is it my fault that I don't care, or is this the system's fault for not inspiring me? What do you think?

As for people at school, *YAWN*. They're all the same; girls trying to be popular so the boys will like them, boys trying to be funny and good at sport so the girls will like them. It's so fake. What kind of world do we live in? C'mon, can't everybody just be themselves? I hope the real world outside of school is not like this. I am who I am and I certainly won't change just to 'fit in'. I have more respect for myself than changing for people just to like me.

It's sad really, I see it every day with girls in my year group. One day they're nice and polite and friendly to each other. But then 'the change' happens. Suddenly those nice and polite friends of yours start hanging out with a different group of girls, the 'it' girls, who only care about makeup and boys and whatever their social media influencers tell them to care about. They have lost their own personalities and are now societal conformists, soulless sheep doing as the flock does. Girls, if you are reading this, please don't change just to fit in. If people cannot accept you for who you are, then are they really worth it? I don't think so!

STUDY: What's it all about? Does it deserve all the fuss it gets? Erm, I'm not so sure. I simply don't like it. Actually, I don't get it. Is it reading a book? Is it taking notes? Is it memorising facts? It's probably all of the above, but I simply struggle to do it. I'm getting better now, but in my previous years, I didn't have a clue what to do. In fact, not once was I ever shown how to study. In school, we learned from the teacher, but nobody actually ever sat me down and said, "OK Sarah, let me show you how to study. Let me show you how to maximise your time in order to make your study time valuable." Nah, this never happened. Shame, it would have helped me!

I tried, I really did, but because I actually didn't know 'how' to study, I was simply reading page after page, but nothing was sinking in. In fact, I remember in my first year of secondary school when we had our exams. For my English test, I simply read the novel we completed in class. I sat in my bedroom day after day reading. I thought I was studying and making an honest effort. ONE question came up on this topic and it was only worth THREE marks! Seriously, three marks for days of intense study? Was I getting the most out of my time? No! Could I have been utilising my time more efficiently? Of course. If only I knew the skills of studying.

HOMEWORK: I hate doing it. I mean, what a waste of time. We spend 8+ hours in school and then we are asked to do more school work at home. Home is called home for a reason. When am I supposed to watch Netflix? When do I walk my dog? When do I play with my friends and when do I get to relax? Talk about dominating my life! I can't work at school all day and then have the energy and focus to do school work at home too. A break is what I need, just give me a break!

What about this for an idea: NO HOMEWORK! Imagine coming home from school and actually having time to yourself. If I get a break at home, then my mind will be fresh and focused for school. If I focus more in school, then I can engage more and be fully present. I will learn more! My grades will improve! Dare I say it, I might even go to university! That's it, genius, simple! Do you know what I mean? Is this such a bad idea? It would certainly work for me. I have tried to express this previously to my teachers and parents. If only people would *listen* to me!

EXAMS: Like study, I have never learned how to sit an exam. I'm improving but, when I think back to when I was younger, I just used to answer every question on the sheet. It was silly really. If I got a paper that said to answer three out of the five questions, I would always answer all five. I'm not sure why. I suppose my philosophy was that I would answer them all and the teacher would select my best three. But would she actually do that? I was wasting valuable time too. If I'd only answered three questions, then I would have had more time on each one, giving my answers more consideration and probably getting better marks. Bizarrely, no teacher ever said this to me, nobody ever pulled me up on this. I kind of figured it out for myself that I was doing it wrong. Maybe I should have known, maybe it's obvious. Or maybe, just maybe, it was someone's responsibility!

Have you ever left an exam thinking you did well but ended up doing poorly? I did, it happened so often. After the exam, everybody would be talking about it, and of course I'd be feeling great and bragging about how easy it was. Then the results would come in, and, yeah, I'd feel stupid!

See, the thing about exams is that the intelligent kids just got on with it, said nothing and received good marks, whereas the arrogant kids like me celebrated the ease of the test, and then abruptly fell back down to earth with a bang when we collected our answer sheet with many, many red pen marks. This was never good news. The red pen was the sign of trouble, trouble at school and trouble at home!

I used to say, "I just wish the teacher would sit me down and show me how it should be done, show me how to successfully answer a question paper." Unfortunately this never happened.

If only people would *listen* to me!

MY SUBJECTS: Some I enjoy and some I despise. I admit, the ones I don't like I don't try hard enough in. Science; it just goes over my head. My Science teacher once told me, "Sarah, Science is everything and everywhere. Every profession involves Science. If you don't get good grades in Science, then you will never get a job."

I hope that's not true. I'm not good at Science. Does this mean I don't have a future?

As I get older, I am beginning to realise that it's no good just focusing on the subjects I like. It's strange really. My school days are up and down. I go into one class, let's say Art, and yeah, I'm happy. Then I move to Maths and, as always, I switch off, not interested whatsoever. After that, I go to PE and I'm in heaven, then off to DT and my day is perfect, I'm fulfilled, I'm satisfied. However, the downside to this magical 'second half of the day' is that the next day comes and I've already had two of my favourite subjects this week.

This means tomorrow is bad, really bad. I don't want to go in. I hate it. I'm not interested one bit!

I tell myself that this attitude needs to change. If I could only get through these lessons, make some sort of an effort to enjoy them and then I might improve. Yes, if I do OK in the subjects I don't like, and really good in the subjects I do like, then my end results should be…relatively OK I suppose. But I know that If I do well in the ones I like, and poor in the ones I don't like, then there is no hope for me. No hope of getting the job that I want. I need something to change, I need to have a new strategy, a new mindset and a new perspective of these subjects. Yes, I admit I don't want them in my life. But they are, they are part of it and I simply need to deal with it. The battle is on!

Points to consider:

- Who do you think is responsible for Sarah's education?

- What is Sarah's perspective now?

- What was the outcome after her change of attitude?

- Did Sarah give herself justification for approaching the subjects she doesn't like with a new state of mind?

- In the end, Sarah comes up with her own conclusion on how she feels about school. What did you notice in her tone of voice when compared to the beginning of the story?

What does the CMB Wellbeing Warrior say?

From your experience at school, what do you consider the best resource to be? Who do you learn best from?

There are so many resources in the classroom beyond the teacher, the books and the internet. You just need to think outside the box! I have said it many times as a teacher, the best resources in the classroom are the students, a room filled with fearless brains full of imagination, creativity, ambition and ideas. We can learn so much from each other when we put our heads together!

During a coaching session with Sarah, this is something we could explore further. This can be achieved in the *CMB Ultimate Companion Recipe*, where we would look at the people around Sarah and identify their skills and characteristics and see how they can add value to the situations Sarah finds herself in. This 'recruitment' can be referred to as 'Sarah's allies', and essentially it is a resource that she can call upon when needing additional support.

For example, let's say Sarah's classmate Anna is really good at Science. Sarah could approach Anna and ask for support, tips or guidance. She could look at Anna's behaviour in Science class to see what she does well, see what is working for her and attempt to model this behaviour. I'm not saying that Sarah should change who she is and copy Anna, rather I'm encouraging her to see what works well for Anna and explore using these skills herself. It's natural for people to pick up other people's characteristics from observing their behaviours. It's like shifting her mindset towards that of Anna and conditioning her behaviour to something that works better.

Over time, Sarah will find that through this small change of behaviour and adapting her new approach towards her Science class, she will begin to see improvements and will be on her way to achieving her personal goals. Once Sarah starts to see small improvements, she will then create an appetite for more. Through this connection and newfound drive towards her Science lessons, anything is now possible for Sarah.

A word of warning however: it is important to think carefully when selecting your allies and make sure they will add value to you and your end goal. You don't want the opposite to happen! The key here is that they must have a positive influence on you, not a negative one!

A second area I would focus on is to take Sarah's new appreciation for Science and expand it into other subjects. We can amplify her new behaviours across other areas that need attention with this new approach.

Ultimately, we want Sarah to apply herself fully to those subjects she struggles with. If she internalises her objective, then she will find a real purpose to change her attitude across all lessons. Have a look at the *'Self Determination Theory'* from Deci and Ryan; it will support you in understanding and applying this methodology.

Through using this approach, the idea is that Sarah will be internally motivated and committed to all her subjects, where she can relate the significance of them to her personal goal, which, in this case, is getting the best results possible.

Sarah identifies that she needs to do 'OK' in the subjects she doesn't like, to achieve this end goal. It's OK not to like every subject in school; students rarely engage in each lesson with equal enthusiasm. However, this does not give one free rein to slack off! Sarah accepts that she does not need to love these subjects or even get top marks; she is saying that she needs to improve and get by. This is a fair perspective. It is an 'achievable' goal, a 'realistic' one, and because of this, it gives Sarah an inner drive to do it. Through further exploration via the *CMB Powerful Process Approach*, we would examine the situation and discuss her goals in order to bring some light to the situation. This process involves deep thought, but in short, we would discuss the desired end product, the feelings associated with accomplishing such goals and create a model that is step by step based, where Sarah can closely monitor its success.

When creating your goals, it is key to prepare a plan that works with you and your way of doing things. This may involve rewards, the inclusion of a friend for accountability purposes, or simply patting yourself on the back after each milestone. The key is to monitor and evaluate your approach, to ensure a successful outcome.

Regarding Sarah's exams and ability to answer her papers, we would explore what Sarah's options are. For example, through this exploration, she could find options such as approaching the teacher and explaining to her how she feels. In this instance, if the teacher knows that this is a challenge for Sarah, she may be willing to sit her down and go over it step by step. It seems that Sarah may need this. Once done, Sarah now has a skill for life. We could then focus on other aspects of Sarah's schooling, or life in general, where these skills can be used.

Throughout her story, Sarah routinely blames others for her failures, thereby negating her own shortcomings. Furthermore, Sarah seems reluctant to ask for help. We are all responsible for our own actions and, unless we ask for help, people don't know there is a problem. Many people in your life will help you, they just need to know what the issue is. Get it out there, make the first move and talk to those who can help you. Most people will want to support you and see you succeed, and those who don't, well, you probably wouldn't ask them in the first place anyway!

Enquiry Question:

If Sarah can figure out that doing well in Science is much bigger than her enjoyment of the lesson, what other aspects of her life can she apply this thinking to?

CMB Task:

Can you identify a current problem in your life? Who do you know has the skills to deal with this? Would you be willing to approach them for help? If you're not sure, ask yourself, is the outcome worth it?!

6

Fabiana: The Bus Bully And My Imaginary Friend

Hi, my name is Fabiana. The relationship I have with school is quite confusing. At times I love it and enjoy being with my friends, and then there are other times where I really want to be anywhere else but school. I feel that people don't get me, especially those in my year, or maybe I just don't get them!

When I'm on the school bus, I sit quietly near the front whilst my friends try to impress the older students, acting weird and out of character just to 'fit in'. I say sit quietly, because when I dare to speak up about how stupid they sound, I just get abuse from the older ones, especially from a boy called Zain.

Zain is the bus bully. He dominates everything and all the other people on the bus are clearly scared of him. Because of this they laugh at his jokes, agree with everything he says and dismiss anyone else's opinion. One time he called Ms. Donnelly a t**t and everyone laughed, which annoyed me, because she's a teacher who is usually well respected. In fact, everybody always wants to be in her class. If she comes in to cover a lesson we all start cheering! So she is very liked. But, because Zain called her a t**t, everybody felt the need to laugh!

Ms. Donnelly has been very good to me and always helps me after lessons and *listens* to me, so I felt that I needed to stick up for her and say something. I said to Zain, "You are wrong, she is not a t**t, she is a lovely person, don't call her that."

Finally, somebody has the guts to stand up to Zain, and it's me! It's time to break the mould and take him down a peg or two. All I need now is for the rest of the bus to have my back. They know I'm right, and this is their chance to show it. I've enabled them! Who's with me?

Silence on the bus. Nobody moves a muscle. They all sit quietly, heads down. Then, a ripple of giggles from one or two people, who must be thinking, *Wow Fabiana, what did you just do?!*

> Ms. Donnelly has been very good to me and always helps me after lessons and *listens* to me, so I felt that I needed to stick up for her and say something.

Zain stands up. He looks at me, his face contorted with anger and hate, one that only a mother could love. And here it goes:

"What do you know you little p***k?! SIT DOWN you pathetic child."

Now, I'm sure you'd agree that this isn't normal behaviour. Rational, well-adjusted human beings don't talk like this. Either way, I'm trapped in a situation I've never been in before. I'm frightened, shaking and, to make matters worse, all of the attention is on me. I need support here, someone to step in and back me up, the same way I was backing our teacher.

But no…more silence.

Zain's not done with me yet. "How dare you challenge me, get off this bus now," he says with chilling calmness. What do I do now? Nobody on the bus is helping me! I could ask the bus driver to say something, but that will only make things worse.

I sit still. Zain sits beside me. He pinches my leg and says, "I will make your life a mess, unless you do as I say. When the bus stops you better get off, or else."

Or else what? I'm wondering. What have I gotten myself into? I only wanted to defend my nice teacher and now something bad is going to happen to me. This isn't fair! Why is nobody stepping in here?

The bus stops. I get off. Great, now I'm standing at a dingy bus stop, miles from the school, on a dark and freezing December morning. I'm going to be late, which means I'll be in trouble. It's not even 8am and today has been a disaster.

I look up at the sky. It's getting darker; rain clouds are forming. Then it pours and, just my luck, I don't even have a coat! The rain is pelting down and puddles are developing near my feet. I'm wet; wet hair, wet feet, simply wet all over. Christ, this is a mess!

The bus schedule is behind a plastic screen, marked with cigarette burns and glazed with rain water. I wipe my hand across it; thankfully, the next bus is heading in the direction of my school. As it approaches I can see that it is full and…yes, you have guessed it, the driver doesn't even stop; he drives on by as if I am invisible. Now I have to wait for the next bus. Plenty of time for the rain to soak me completely!

When I finally get to school, I have to sign in at reception and explain to the battleaxe receptionist why I am late and why I am wet. Why do school receptionists think that they are the police? It's like an interrogation! Anyway, I lie and say that I missed my original bus, then got caught in the rain. No sense in telling the truth; what would be the point? I spoke my truth on the bus when I stood up to Zain, and look where that got me!

I trudge down the school hall, a physical and emotional wreck. I'm trying to appear calm and collected, but I'm not much of an actor. When I enter the classroom, my teacher can clearly see that I am distressed. He knows something isn't right. He keeps probing me, asking what's wrong. I just want to be left alone, some time to myself to get my thoughts together. I need space, not questions. "Just leave me alone," I growl under my breath.

I'm sitting at the school desk, head down, hands pressed into my temples. The teacher is talking to me, but I have completely shut down. I have now sat there for over 30 minutes and have refused to engage with him or the class. Thankfully, he gives me the space I am craving and leaves me alone.

The lesson is now over and everybody is leaving. I'm still in a strange place emotionally. I want to talk to the teacher, but I feel safe tucked into my arms, I feel protected from the outside world. The teacher is now getting understandably frustrated, as he doesn't know what to do and the next class is now arriving. He calls another student over. "Go and get Mr. Smith," he tells him.

Mr. Smith is my Head of Year, a lovely man who has always been there for me and my mother, whether I had issues at school or at home. He comes in and sits beside me. He speaks softly to me, his gentle approach always creates a calm atmosphere. I like him, he is a good person and I have a lot of respect for him.

I eventually lift my head. He asks if we can go somewhere private to talk about what's wrong. We find an empty room, but I'm still not ready to talk. What can I say? If I tell the truth, Zain will get in trouble, which will mean trouble for me. If I lie, it'll look like I'm having a breakdown, which will mean spending time with the school counsellor. I don't want that, it'll just get people gossiping about my mental state. I'm really not sure what to do. Maybe I should just tell the truth. Ah, but the incident occurred on a public bus, so the police might get involved, and then I'll need to make an official statement at the station! For goodness sake, what do I do?

OK, decision time: let's bring Sasha into this! Good old Sasha, she never lets me down. Nobody knows how to deal with this chestnut so this is my way out. I have no other choice, it's a last resort. Here goes...

I sit up, take a deep breath and tell Mr. Smith, "My best friend from primary school died a few years ago, and today's the anniversary of her death. Her name was Sasha, and I really miss her. Every year, on the anniversary of her death, I tend to lose control of myself and simply fall apart."

Silence. Mr. Smith doesn't respond, he just sits there, in a daze. I've surprised him. I wait for the clichéd responses, something along the lines of, *Oh, I'm so sorry! Take all the time you need!* Then I'm left alone, I regain my composure and I'm fine for the rest of the day. That's how it usually goes.

Not this time!

"Tell me all about Sasha," he says.

WHAT?! I wasn't expecting that! He wants to know everything about Sasha, who she was, what she looked like and what she meant to me as a friend. I have never been asked these questions before.

I'm in trouble. Can you guess why? Yeah: 'Sasha' isn't real! I made her up, to get me out of situations like this. So now I'm reeling off lie after lie, and I feel terrible for doing so. Please Mr. Smith, stop with the 21 questions already!

Just as I think that this situation cannot get any worse, he asks me to close my eyes and 'complete a visualisation'. "You gotta be joking," I whisper to myself, but I do as he asks and shut my eyes tight.

"Imagine you are with Sasha now, any place, but somewhere you have been together, fully immerse yourself in this place and moment." A few minutes later, he says, "Now open your eyes and tell me all about it!"

OMG, this is certainly an experience for Sasha and I like no other. I understand what Mr. Smith is trying to do here. He is trying to get me to relive special moments I have had with Sasha. He is celebrating our relationship, as opposed to dwelling on her death. This hole I'm in is getting bigger and bigger and I'm still digging!

Mr. Smith has been with me for over an hour now, and I feel really guilty. Should I come clean? What would you do?

I chicken out. I invent a story about me and Sasha on holiday together. I talk about where we went, what we did, everything. Mr. Smith tells me how brave I am to express it all, and how lucky Sasha was to have a friend like me. Eventually, I say I'm feeling much better, that I'm in a good place mentally. Mr. Smith is happy with this and lets me go. It took a while, but it worked. Good old Sasha to the rescue as usual, never in doubt!

Wow, what a day this has been. Finally, I get home and look forward to a nice, relaxing evening away from all the trouble today has brought. "Hi Mum," I say. Mum smiles, looks at me and says, "Hi Fabiana…who is Sasha?"

Points to consider:

- Regarding Zain and the bus incident, did Fabiana make the correct decision confronting him? What do you think she was expecting him to say? Do you think Fabiana's desired outcome was achievable?

- Could the school receptionist have done more to help Fabiana? If so, what?

- What are your thoughts on 'Sasha'? Was Fabiana justified in mentioning her imaginary friend to Mr. Smith? How might he feel if or when he discovers the truth?

- Imagine the conversation Fabiana had with her mum after the story ended; how do you think it went?

What does the CMB Wellbeing Warrior say?

Like many coaching conversations, a client will bring a plethora of possible agendas to the table. This is fine. However, in order for a coach to support their client efficiently, we need to whittle down the actual topic for today. A great question here would be: "Fabiana, what would a good outcome be after our session?"

In this instance, the client will stop giving random pieces of information (or letting off steam) and begin to think deeper about what they want to discuss in the session. Once the response is given, a probing question, such as, "What will this look like?" can come in handy, as it gives the coach a visual of what the client wants to see.

Clearly, the bullying from Zain is a major topic here. However, let's say that, through some powerful questions, Fabiana has expressed that the involvement of Sasha in her life is confusing her and starting to have a negative impact on her life, then this is where the coaching conversation shall go, if that's what Fabiana wants of course!

As always, we would explore the agenda and discuss 'Sasha' and her involvement in Fabiana's life. At no stage would I suggest that this all sounds a bit silly or childish. Coaching is a partnership between the coach and the client and involves a relationship without the presence of judgement, as mentioned previously. By making this clear, the path is free for Fabiana to openly discuss her affiliation with Sasha.

Statements from coach to client to form agreements such as: "There will be no involvement of judgement in our coaching sessions," "This is a safe place to express whatever you need," and, "At any point during our coaching conversations, if you feel uncomfortable, please just let me know and we can press pause," are created through the *CMB Red Carpet Compromise Creator*.

These agreements are key to the success of the relationship between the coach and the client, as it demonstrates a level of trust and expectations from both parties on how the sessions will be conducted. Once agreements are constructed and there is a clear and mutual understanding, then the foundations are in place for a successful coaching session.

Involving agreements at the start of any relationship is a wonderful tool in order to create the correct environment to proceed with a shared vision. I personally conduct them with all the school classes I teach, no matter what age they are, and with every client I have when coaching.

Creating agreements builds a perfect base for a successful partnership, both professionally and even personally! A simple question like, "Tell me what you want from me," provides you with useful information on how to conduct yourself with the other person. It also works twofold, as you can then express how you want others to behave in the relationship towards you. Many coaches and leaders in a range of different industries would use a method such as this to support them when dealing with the performance of individuals or teams.

A key ingredient to successful agreements is flexibility. They are not rules and are not set in stone. They are <u>expectations</u>, which will be monitored and adapted if and when required.

Once the agreements are created, then the coaching journey would proceed. A question such as, "Fabiana, where do you want to start?" will provide her with the control needed to kick-start her own road to success.

Enquiry Questions:

Many of us have been in the situation where we choose to look away as opposed to engaging or confronting bad behaviour, even though we know what we see is wrong. If you were on the bus and you witnessed Fabiana confronting Zain, what would you have done? What would have been the consequences for you for choosing to do this?

eMB Task:

Select an area of your life where agreements could be implemented to support the objective. With the person (or people) involved, cooperatively create the agreements that you would all like to include. Observe the outcome and adapt if needed. Remember, it needs to work for all parties involved to be successful.

7

Livia: Dad, Please listen!

My name is Livia and my story is about bullying.

I guess bullying was a big part of my life, as it happened continuously when I joined my new school. It was one girl called Kira. You see, Kira was a very dominant and nasty person. Everybody was afraid of her, even the teachers!

Kira clearly got her attitude from home. Every time there was a problem at school, or when she was in trouble, her parents would come in, 'tell the teacher off' and take Kira's side, all the time. Yes, you heard that correctly! I saw the way they spoke to the teacher. Shockingly, one day they confronted him in front of the class, asking why it's always Kira in trouble and what is he doing to support her. They even questioned his teaching credentials one time. I mean, how embarrassing for the teacher. There was clearly no respect. I'm not surprised Kira behaved the way she did, she thought she was untouchable!

Regarding the bullying from her, it was emotional and physical bullying. Kira, ugh, I really hate using her name, 'she' made my life hell. I wanted out of this school so much but my parents didn't see how badly it was affecting me. They just wouldn't *listen!*

I moved into this new school when my dad had to relocate for work purposes. On the first day I arrived I was so excited, a new start.

The night before I started I lay on my bed, looking up to the ceiling in the dark and imagining the next day and how wonderful it would be. Who will be my teacher? What will the uniform look like on me? Who will my friends be and most of all…who will my new best friend be?! I literally couldn't sleep, I kept checking the time every hour, wishing the night away.

The next morning I met my form teacher, a lovely lady with a strange accent; French I think. She had a gentle approach and my first thoughts were positive. I felt in good hands. She asked me to introduce myself to the class.

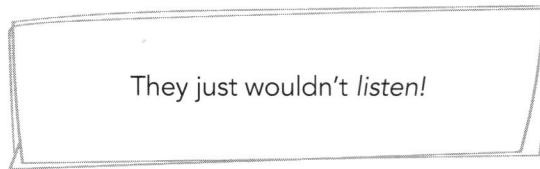

They just wouldn't *listen!*

"Hi all, my name is Livia and I am from Brazil…"

Straight away I realised what my biggest problem would be. The boys started whistling, smiling and shouting, but the girls were all looking at me like…*Who does this new girl think she is?*

Sitting in front of me was a large girl, chewing gum, with a horrible golden necklace and rings all over her fingers. She just stared at me throughout. This was Kira, and I could tell that this was not good!

As we moved into our next lesson, the boys were all around me asking questions: "What's it like in Brazil?" "When did you come here?" "Do you have a boyfriend?" that sort of thing. You name it, they asked it! OK, so I was getting attention. I knew I was different as I am Brazilian and I have always had boys interested in me, but this was a new level. I felt like a celebrity, I really did.

In our next class, I was sitting down quietly doing my work and I could see Kira staring at me. I was like, "Hey," but she just kept staring. I was now getting uncomfortable. When the teacher asked the class a question, Kira shouted out, "Ask the Brazilian, or should I say Mrs. Popular."

Now, I knew I had a problem!

The next lesson was PE. In the changing room, I made sure I sat away from Kira. I got changed as quickly as I could as, at this stage, I felt uneasy and frightened.

For our lesson, we were doing a stepping exercise on the benches. It was some kind of physical test. I was wearing my own leggings, as I didn't have the correct PE kit yet. In hindsight I should not have worn them; they were too tight and they got me too much attention. I suppose they didn't leave too much to the imagination!

The boys sat behind me and were clearly checking me out. I was now very uncomfortable, but I didn't know what to do. I know this all sounds like I'm playing the victim card and that I was soaking up the attention, but it really wasn't like that. It was quite unpleasant to be perfectly honest.

The teacher Mr. Taylor noticed that I was uneasy and what the boys were playing at. You could say they were 'boys being boys', but remember, this was my first day and I didn't know what they were capable of.

Mr. Taylor was nice and calm. He got the boys to move and leave me alone. Unfortunately for me, the damage was already done. I could see Kira from a distance, again eyeballing me, major jealousy was kicking in and I could sense trouble was coming my way.

Apparently, she is quite 'close' to many of the boys. She clearly didn't like that I was getting attention from the boys that she 'entertains' regularly. You can work that one out for yourself!

The lesson was now over and it was time to get changed. Picture this…a school changing room crowded with girls getting changed. Some nice pleasant girls, some sporty girls, some popular chatty girls, and, of course…Kira.

Bizarrely, she started singing loudly. It was 'noise' more than singing; I couldn't help but look at her. She reacted, "What are you looking at Brazilian?"

I didn't respond.

"Hey b***h, don't go quiet on me! What are you looking at?"

"I'm not looking at anything," I replied.

"What are you trying to say?" Kira asked. I didn't respond. "I'll punch you, I really will," she said.

She walked over and literally punched me in the face. I was in shock; I had never been physically hit before. She grabbed my school bag and emptied it out. My books, my makeup and my phone all fell to the floor. She stood over me and said, "How are you now, Mrs. Pretty?" She took my phone and walked away.

At lunchtime, I didn't know what to do, or where to go. I was hungry, but I didn't want to go to the canteen in case Kira was there. I looked out of the window to the grey sky and rain pelting against the window pane. As I stood there I could see my cold breath on the glass. Please, please, please, get me out of here, get me home. I missed my old life, my old school and my best friend, Maria. I needed Maria by my side right now.

I walked around the school to explore it, but also to stay clear of Kira. There was now ten minutes to go, so I guessed the canteen was empty. I cautiously went in and looked at the menu. There was not much food left! Ah, pasta. "Can I have some pasta with sauce please?" I asked the nice canteen lady. It was served in a cardboard cup. I grabbed my plastic fork and attempted to eat it. The pasta was so overcooked it literally melted in my mouth, and the sauce was like water with red bits floating in it. Let's just say it wasn't the most nourishing or aesthetically pleasing meal I have ever had. Could this day get any worse? You'd better believe it!

My next lesson was Art. The teacher was an old lady, grumpy and old-fashioned. Peculiarly, she seemed to have a good relationship with Kira, in fact too good of a relationship. Kira appeared to be the boss of this class. "Kira, can you do this?" "Kira, can you do that?" "Kira, ask the class to be quiet," and guess what, the class was quiet. I was sitting there wondering what kind of place this is. How could a student have more control than a teacher? Strange, to say the least!

I still needed to get my phone back so, as Kira seemed to be in a good mood in this lesson, I thought I would ask her. Politely, I said, "Hi Kira, can I please have my phone back?" Embarrassingly, she laughed in my face. To make it worse, out of the blue in the middle of the class, she actually spat on me. Honestly, she did. I have never felt so disgusted. This place was just a disaster. I needed to get out of there quickly, it felt worse than prison!

I went to my seat and rubbed the spit off my face with the sleeve of my school jumper. I didn't show it but I was screaming inside; I had never felt so alone in my life. I couldn't stay here, I really couldn't.

I didn't want to tell the teacher as I didn't want to make it worse. After all, it seemed her and Kira had a special relationship. I eventually got out and went home.

What next? I really didn't know. Should I tell my parents? We didn't usually have these kinds of conversations and our relationship was not very open. However, I was in so much emotional pain that I needed to do something. I literally could not go back to school tomorrow. I felt that if I told them they may feel guilty for moving here. My mind was racing. One minute I agreed with myself to tell them and then the next I talked myself out of it. Have you ever experienced this?

I had become an emotional wreck. I was afraid to leave my room and wallowing in an indecisive state. My head was not right, not in a good place. This awful day was too much for me. I was all completely flustered.

Hours, literally *hours* later, I stood up, looked in the mirror and said to myself, "OK…here goes, you need to do this Livia."

I went downstairs and sat in the kitchen, where my father was doing the dishes. The air reeked of lemon washing up liquid. It was a dark, miserable evening, and there was an old-style fire range in the room. I could feel the raw heat of it on my face as I sat there practising what to say over and over in my head.

I took a big deep breath.

Me: Dad, I've had a hard time at school today.

Silence

Me: Dad, did you hear me?

Dad: Ah, yeah, it can't be easy in a new school and a new country.

Me: No dad it's not, a girl, Kira is giving me trouble.

More silence. Dad hasn't even turned away from the sink

Me: (Slightly louder) Dad, she has made my day a misery.

Dad: Don't worry, it will blow over soon.

Me: (Even louder) Dad, she punched me, she spat on me and she took my phone.

Silence again. Dad's giving me nothing

What should I do now? I had hoped he would understand, but he didn't. I looked out of the window feeling drained from it all, broken even. I couldn't do this any longer. What else was there to do? I tried to talk but he was not listening. He didn't want to hear what I had to say.

It was last resort time now. I walked over and physically turned him around to face me. I looked deeply into his eyes and I burst out crying right in front of him.

Now, he 'saw' me, I finally got his attention.

Points to consider:

- Regarding the first day of school, could Livia have taken any responsibility?

- Livia mentioned that she missed her friend Maria. Are there any resources available to connect with Maria, even though she might not be living in the same country?

- Can you imagine what Livia is about to say to her father at the end?

- What do you think her dad is experiencing and how may he be feeling?

- What did Livia do that got his attention?

- Is he the bad person here for not listening?

- What advice would you like to give to Livia and her dad?

What does the CMB Wellbeing Warrior say?

There are any number of possible topics in this story. There are Livia's expectations on her first day of school, Kira the bully, reasons for not informing the teachers of what is happening, missing home, her friend Maria and finding it challenging to express her feelings to her father, to name a few.

At the start of the story, Livia has built a whole picture of what her perfect first day at her new school will be like. She mentions her new best friend and how she will look in her uniform. This is all hypothetical of course, as she is forecasting this image in her mind.

In coaching, we use the phrase 'truths', which can be developed in the *CMB Proven Truth Tactic*. This essentially describes how we believe the world works, based on our experiences and examples previously set out to us. Our truths can be determined by our 'nature', which can be traits inherited from our parents or our 'nurture', such as the experiences we had exercised.

Your 'truths' are personal and will differ from person to person. Here are some typical examples:

- Everybody is equal
- You get what you deserve in life
- Treat people how they treat you

Now, have a think about what life would be like if you followed each of these identified truths. Let's just say, I don't think it would be straightforward. Can you recognise how they may cause you problems?

This is why, when creating your own 'truths', it takes deep thought and time to get them right. Sometimes we get our truths wrong, and if we hold onto them they can have severe consequences to how we feel and behave.

In Livia's story, she builds this fantasised version of what her first day 'should' be like. This could be influenced by past experiences. By using a more cautious approach through the skills learned when a client designs their own 'truths', Livia could create a new perception of what her day 'could' be like. With this new, safer way of thinking, Livia now has the ammunition to protect her expectations when she feels that things have not gone as planned. Through this lens, she is better prepared to deal with it. Of course, I am not suggesting that this makes it all better, but it will go some way in allowing herself to feel victimised.

Regarding Livia's dad. I would understand if you feel that he is ignoring her and not 'being there' for his daughter. I hear this many times, "If only my mother did this," "I wish my dad was like that," or "Why can't my parents be like my friends' parents?" and so on.

In coaching, we don't blame; it's not helpful and offers no development for the client. It's common for teenagers to start off on their coaching journey through the eyes of a victim.

On this occasion, I would certainly empathise with Livia, but as a coach, it is essential not to go down the path of the 'blame game'. Instead, we can get her to understand her dad and appreciate how this must feel for him. Remember, we don't know what he is going through here.

In this instance, from the outside looking in, it is clear that Livia's father is uncomfortable with having this type of conversation. In fact, Livia has expressed that: 'We don't have an open relationship'. We cannot force these things and the reality is that we are all distinctive and come from different generations, hence we cannot expect to have the same skillset.

In a coaching session, a possible avenue would be to focus on dad's perspective and gain an appreciation for the difficulties he is also experiencing here. This doesn't mean that the topic is about dad. The focus is still on Livia and her feelings about her dad. Through this approach, Livia would then find an appreciation for her father's behaviour and instead of feeling that he is not there for her, accept his style of behaviour, and explore other means of breaking down this communication barrier. Essentially, Livia needs to treat her father the way 'he' needs to be treated in order for him to be able to support her. It's a team effort, where they will see progress through communicating cohesively. Being able to change perspective is a very powerful skill, and we will touch on this topic later in the book.

Enquiry Question:

Put yourself in Livia's shoes. Using her new behavioural perspective when communicating with her father, think of the best sentence that she could come up with in order to start the conversation. Remember, she needs to demonstrate her pain, but also to get through to her dad the way he will understand.

CMB Task:

Task 1: Reflect on yourself and how approachable you are. Do you possess welcoming traits or unwelcoming traits? Think about when people approach you to express how they feel. How have you responded? What skills did you use? What was the outcome? If the outcome was discouraging, what could you do differently the next time someone approaches you with a concern?

Task 2: What are your 'truths'? Set aside some time to yourself and give your truths the minutes, or hours, they deserve. List them and see how they are impacting the way you behave. Remember, if they are not having a positive impact then try and let them go, they are not serving you!

8

Jo: I Just Want To Be Me

I have always had a feminine taste. From an early age, I loved things that were 'meant for girls'. So, as expected, I had a hard time with this. Not everybody understood me. Not everybody knew the pain and torment they put me through.

My name is Jo and I'm a boy. My school life has been one of many challenges, all because I cannot be accepted for who I am and who I want to be. Here is my story.

As I said, I have a feminine taste, and I'm OK with this. I prefer girls clothes, I like to hang out with girls and I like to do 'girly' things, or should I say things that society believes are girly.

It all started when I was very young. In primary school, we were doing a drama activity where we had to dress up as characters from our stories. We could choose any costume we wanted. There was a range of different costumes in a big wooden cabinet in the school cloakroom, from sports clothes to ancient Roman togas. I assumed they were clothes collected by the teacher over the years for this particular activity at school, possibly donated. Mmm…reflecting back, I hope they were washed!

I enjoy dressing up, so I'm really excited as I'm reaching into this gigantic cabinet and picking out clothes for my character 'Jessie'. *Sweater, NO. Jeans, NO. An old man's cardigan…I don't think so!*

Ah, a lovely aquamarine dress! I grab it quickly and, without any consideration or judgement from myself, I put it on.

This was the start of my school life troubles. Even to this day, I describe it as *'Doomsday'*. It was the beginning and the end of the feminine Jo in school and the start of me being classified as 'different'.

That same day during break time, a group of boys in an older year group came up to me and asked, "Are you the boy that wore a dress?"

I didn't know what to say, and this was in a lunch hall where everybody could see everything. They kept at it: "Hahahaha, you're a girl! You're a girl! You're a girl!" and so on. I was literally speechless as I was just standing there all alone. I felt numb and started crying.

At this age, I wasn't sure what the problem was, but my teacher did. Miss Higgins could obviously sense that I had somewhat distinctive tastes when compared to the other boys. I'm sure she was a lovely person, but back then when I was so young we felt that she was a big monster. We were so afraid of doing the wrong thing and getting in trouble. I wasn't confident enough to approach her and explain how I was feeling. The relationship just wasn't strong enough.

After the dress incident and further instances of me selecting girl groups over boy groups when doing class activities, Miss Higgins called my parents into school and expressed a 'concern'. She said that I wore a dress and that she felt that I was prone to hanging out with the girls more than the boys. She identified that I was 'different'. Ugh, how is this word so negative?! Miss Higgins said that there was nothing wrong with this, but wanted to alert my parents in case it was something they needed to know.

But to me, it felt like there was something wrong. Why call my parents in? I just wore a dress, right? And what's wrong with hanging out with girls? They are human beings and they are nicer to me than the boys, so of course I prefer to be in their company.

Then things escalated. Other parents began to talk and ask questions. "What is going on with him?" "What are his parents thinking?" "Why wear them girly clothes?" and so on. That last comment was sent my way on a non-uniform day. I wore a pink t-shirt. Is this really a sin? What kind of world do we live in?

At this stage, I felt like it was an attack on me, on who I am, or who I was trying to be. I overheard my parents talking about it. It wasn't easy for them either. Each attack on me was an attack on them.

My parents always backed me. They are great, they *listen* to me. I am blessed to have such an open and understanding family who get me, and this gives me hope that others eventually will too. You see, at home, I can be me, Jo 'the girl'. Outside I am who society wants me to be, Jo 'the boy'. Confused? Of course you are. But I'm not confused. I just want to be happy, simple as that. Even now, not everyone gets that, just me, my friends, my family and my teachers. These are the people I trust.

Trust! This is really important for me. One time at school during lunch, my friend Katie (or at least I thought she was my friend) came up to me and said, "Jo, it's OK to be honest with me, please trust me, it's clear that you want to be a girl." Immediately, a massive sensation went through my body, you know, like goosebumps, where the hairs were standing on the back of my neck. I was genuinely so happy, so relieved I wanted to hug her there and then. I took a big deep breath in, exhaled with a massive sigh of relief. Someone finally understood me and who I wanted to be. So, without any consideration, I said "YES" with great confidence. "I'm so not comfortable in this body. I want to be able to express myself and to be honest, I'm happier being a girl."

Oh, the pleasure in just being able to speak out and express how I really felt. I finally had an ally at school, a team-mate who would have my back when the chips were down, right?

I'm afraid it didn't work out this way. Katie got what she came for! Once I had said what I did, she smiled and ran away. Then the penny dropped. *What have I done?* I thought to myself. *What is going to happen now?*

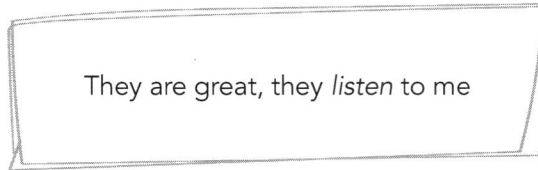

> They are great, they *listen* to me

Moments later, a group of boys came running into the canteen and started singing: "Jo Jo Jo, the boy who wears girl's clothes! The boy who wears girl's clothes! Jo Jo Jo…" and so on. I was mortified, shaken, alone, hurt and angry. Angry with Katie, angry with the boys, angry with society and angry with myself for being so open.

I ran away, through the double-doors, down the corridor and into the toilets. I opened one cubicle; it was filthy. I tried the next one; the floor was wet. Last one. "Please let it be clean," I said to myself.

BINGO! It was clean. I walked in and went to close the door, only to discover that there was no lock! Great, I couldn't even hide away here. So I had to go back to the one with the wet floor and tiptoe my way onto the toilet seat. I put loads of toilet paper over the seat, as it was unsurprisingly dirty. I sat there with my head in my hands, sobbing. This was so unfair, what was wrong with me? I just wanted to be who I wanted to be, couldn't people just get it? What was wrong with wanting this, was it really too much to ask?

I kept asking myself: *why does society have people believing that girls and boys have to be different?* I mean it's 2021! Could I simply not be feminine, like someone is sporty, or arty?

So I sat there, in that cold, horrible, smelly school toilet. Then, some boys walked in. I felt terrified. They started talking very loudly. There was an echo in the room, which made it difficult to hear what they were saying. I listened carefully, and the inevitable happened.

"Did you see Jo run away like that? I cannot believe what happened."

"What a weirdo."

I was now a WEIRDO apparently. I felt humiliated. What was wrong with these people?

What should I do now? It was time to go to my lesson, but the boys were still in the toilets. I couldn't be late for class because everybody would laugh at me as I entered. But I also couldn't open the door, as I could not face these boys. So I sat, and sat, and sat, for fifty-five minutes until the end of the period. The bell eventually rang and I decided that I had had enough.

I ran out of the toilet and straight out of the school gates. I didn't stop running until I reached my front garden. Oh, how happy I was to see my house, my home, where I felt safe. I didn't care if I got into trouble for leaving school without permission, I needed out. I needed to protect myself. I needed to do what was right for me.

I tell my mum everything and, as always, she understands. This is my rock, my family. I could not be me without them. My situation is bad with regards to social acceptance, but at least I have my family. I feel so sorry for those out there in my situation without any family backing.

If I could give any advice to anyone reading this, please don't judge. Allow people to be who they want to be. Let people express themselves and be comfortable in their own skin. School is tough for me, it still is. Not all the time to be fair. I am lucky to have great teachers and friends who understand me. Yes, not everyone does, and this can cause difficult situations. PE is a challenge due to same-sex lessons and the changing room situation, but my teachers accommodate me where possible. In fact, they are very supportive of me. I am very grateful for the lengths they go to, to make it work for me.

Looking back, I'm actually kind of glad these incidents happened in the past, because now I've developed a thick skin and I'm very resilient to insults. It has prepared me for the real world and the challenges I will face in the future.

As a role model of mine who spent their school days just like me said: "It will be hard, but it will be worth it." And I know it will. I know that when I finish school I can rip off my uniform and say goodbye to the shackles of judgement and exclusion from people and look forward to university life, where I know I will be able to express myself exactly the way I want to. Watch out fashion industry, I'm coming for you!

Points to consider:

- How did you feel when Jo finished the story on such a high note?

- What can you learn from Jo on how the situation was managed?

- Jo clearly has a great appreciation for his supportive family; can you imagine what this journey would be like without family support?

- Did Miss Higgins do the right thing calling Jo's parents in? Did this help the situation? What else could Miss Higgins have done to build a more trusting relationship with Jo?

- Regarding the other parents, was their behaviour appropriate? Can you see it from their perspective?

- What would you like to say to Jo right now?

What does the CMB Wellbeing Warrior say?

Some coaching sessions can be a little different than usual, based on the client's personal situation. This is a perfect example, as immediately when you hear Jo's story you ask yourself, "Do I address Jo as a boy or a girl?" I know physiologically Jo is a boy, but remember, we need to be present with the client. As a coach in this instance, it is important to find out how Jo wants to be referred to. Boy or girl? When coaching, we need to leave our own opinions at the door and, if a coach is uneasy with this, then they are not the right fit for Jo. A referral to another coach would be recommended.

From the outset, the first question is significant. A simple question such as, "Jo, please tell me how you would like me to address you," will eliminate any apprehension associated with identity. This will immediately provide the client with the respect they deserve, and in many cases long for.

For the purpose of this story, let's say Jo expressed that he was comfortable being referred to as a boy, therefore I will use the terms 'he' and 'him' when discussing Jo's story.

You can feel the pain Jo has experienced, and is clearly still experiencing. What stands out to you when reading this?

The support from his family is key to Jo getting through the challenges. This support mechanism is fundamental in allowing him to believe; believe that there are people out there who will 'get him', as he so nicely put in his own words.

Jo also mentioned that he has a role model. Did you feel the sense of hope Jo gets for his future when referring to the person he so clearly admires? Once there is hope, anything is possible!

It is always nice to hear a story end so positively, but let's be honest, if we really dig deep and ask Jo some powerful questions, we could expect to unearth a wealth of pain and emotion. This is OK, however, as the journey to real self-belief begins at this point.

For this coaching session, I am going to explore Jo's allies and, through the *CMB Ultimate Companion Recipe*, we will equip him with certain character traits that he can use when experiencing difficult times. We touched on this in Chapter 5 with Sarah, but the approach was somewhat different. This is a perfect example of how the CMB modules can be utilised differently and uniquely with each client.

Firstly, we will look at the people in Jo's inner circle and identify their skills and characteristics. This generally consists of family and close friends. We would go through each person and look at their personality traits in detail, with a view to expose those parts of their personalities that Jo admires. For example, let's say that Jo expressed the following:

"My mother is very calm. When somebody challenges her, she always steps back from the situation, composes herself and proceeds in a manner that is respectful but assertive."

On this occasion, if someone was rude to Jo, instead of getting upset, he could ask himself:

"What would mum do here? She would be calm, so I need to be calm to tackle this behaviour."

Another example for this particular story could come from Jo's outer circle. The outer circle consists of people you don't know personally, but who have an effect on you, like a role model. Let's say Jo's role model is Olympic diver Tom Daley. In this instance, when faced with a challenge, Jo could ask himself:

"What would Tom do right now?"

Of course, this won't always work, but it is one skill that can be called upon to empower a client.

Try it, dip into your inner or outer circle and call upon certain personalities when needed. I like to phrase it as 'borrowing a piece of them for today'!

I personally use this ideology when I'm on stage. I get very nervous when speaking publicly in front of large crowds, and therefore I call upon one of my allies. I 'borrow' Barack Obama's personality traits. Before I step out onto the stage, I visualise how he presents himself and how he makes the audience feel. I simply try to mimic this behaviour, by speaking with confidence, charisma, charm and a warm smile. Thanks Barack!

Back to the story. When faced with a dilemma, Jo decided to run. He said he didn't care if he got into trouble, as he needed to protect himself. "I needed to do what was right for me."

Here, I would commend Jo for making this decision and taking control so assertively. There was clearly a massive sigh of relief when Jo got home. However, the reality is that Jo has avoided the situation, as tomorrow is a new day. It would be important to explore the consequences of this decision and how tomorrow could be tackled.

When we avoid things, we tend to allow ourselves to believe that the situation will take care of itself, and therefore we never get to deal with the real root of the problem. When we get an unpleasant outcome from avoiding a situation, we need to be able to accept the consequences if it doesn't go to plan. This alone is another agenda for another day. We will discuss this in more detail later in the book.

Enquiry Questions:

Imagine you were Jo in the toilets. Think about what was going through his head. Do you open the door and go to class? Do you confront the boys? Or do you sit there and wait and eventually go home as Jo did? What other actions could Jo have taken in order to handle the situation? What would you have done, and what would the expected outcome have been from selecting this option?

CMB Task:

Task 1: Is there anybody in your life right now who is 'different'? Jo has already told us that this word can be used so negatively. Let's change this to a positive meaning. Let's celebrate diversity. In Jo's own words, *'Please don't judge. Allow people to be who they want to be. Let people express themselves and be comfortable in their own skin'*.

Using Jo's advice, what can you do to support those around you who may want to express themselves differently?

Task 2: Design your own allies. Have a think about who your allies are. Who is in your inner and outer circles and identify what traits they have that you can 'borrow'.

Make a list of these selected people, or put each one of them on a PowerPoint/keynote page or somewhere else if you prefer. Include a photo and a list of their personality traits. You can call upon this powerful resource whenever needed.

9

Tariq: The Treacherous Journey Of A Refugee

Assalam Alaikum! Tariq here. I am 17 years old and I am a 'foreigner', apparently! Can you believe that this is my problem, this has been my challenge, being from a different country! Now, before we go into my story, you will have to accept my apologies. My English, although much improved, is still not perfect, so I hope you understand my writing and how I tell this story.

I moved to England when I was 11. My journey to get here was quite the challenge in itself, so this is where I will start. Here it goes.

I grew up in a small house in the countryside in the Middle East. It was me, my five brothers, my two sisters, my mother and my father, all in one room. That's right, ten of us in one room, where we ate and slept. You might think this is hell, but for us, this was heaven. This was home. We had a roof over our heads, we had running water and we had electricity 'some of the time', so all wasn't that bad.

It was a noisy place. Talking, shouting, crying and…bombing. Yes, you heard that right, bombing. This was home, this was war!

When I think back to this time, I remember hearing bombshells above me, whizzing through the air and exploding. One distinct day remains clear in my memory for unfortunate reasons. When I close my eyes I can still see my family and friends running for shelter. It was a dark, dark day for everybody.

On this particular day the shelling was getting closer and closer, louder and louder. Then…a silence and a sense of calmness. Clutching each other, my mother shouts, "ALHAMDULILLAH, ALHAMDULILLAH, ALHAMDULILLAH! We are saved today!"

Then…BANG! A noise like never before comes before us. It's a huge explosion. That's all I remember.

Sometime later I woke up, dazed, confused and in pain. I looked around for my family, among a thick cloud of dust. My father is missing.

"Baba!" I cry out.

Silence.

"Baba?"

Still nothing.

"BABAAAAAAAAA," I scream as loud as I can.

Nothing.

Eventually after some searching my father was dug out of the rubble; he was killed in his own home. A pain like never before hit me, it felt like I was stabbed in the heart.

Thankfully the rest of my family survived; this is all I could hold on to during this difficult time. After my father's funeral, my eldest brother Ziad made a plan. He was now the big man of the house, the head of the family. He decided that it was time to go, to get out of here and away from this mess that we have been born into. We were leaving this war, leaving home for a better life. We are going to England.

My cousins are already in England, they are in school and my uncle is working, so we have a base when we arrive. It is just me and my youngest brother, Mohammed, that are going; Ziad is staying with my mother and other brothers and sisters. I tried to convince them that it would be best for all of us to stick together, but they didn't *listen*. Mum said that she couldn't do it, she wasn't allowing war to force her away from her own home. She wanted to be close to my father also, even though he had passed she couldn't be separated from him. Together until the end she said.

The night before we leave we have some food with the family. My mother is crying, sitting in the corner on her old wooden rocking chair. I go over to her and say, "Mama, please don't worry, we will be OK, I will look after Mohammad and we will make it. We will create a new life in England, a better life. Once we have settled you can come and we will be together again. This is what baba wanted. Home is not safe for us."

As I look deeply into her eyes the truth stares at me in the face. I hug her and say goodbye, goodbye forever potentially.

> I tried to convince them that it would be best for all of us to stick together, but they didn't *listen*.

The morning of the trip we wake up at 4am and there is a stranger at the door. It is an old man, with dark clothes and a wrinkly face. "Go, go, go," he says, "quickly, quickly." He is all flustered and panicky. I'm literally half asleep so I just stand up, grab my bag and leave without any thought. As we drive off into the sunrise I look out the back of the car window. I see my home getting smaller and smaller until it's gone. "Goodbye," I say, as I hide under a blanket and close my eyes.

Hours later we hear noises. The driver is talking to a policeman. We are shaking, what is going to happen? Is this ending before it has begun? Off comes my blanket and I am blinded by the sun as it shines into my eyes. The policeman checks my face and says, "Go, go, go."

This experience is repeated over and over the next couple of days at different checkpoints. I can only leave the car to use the toilet every few hours. When eating I need to stay under the blanket, no talking to Mohammad, nothing, just sitting, sitting, and sitting in the back of a car with the sun beating down on top of us. It is hot, very hot!

Days later and we are still on the road. We have now moved into a larger truck, more like a lorry actually. It is massive, with more people, many more people, mostly boys my age. It smells, it smells real bad. We are given strict instructions not to talk. Just sit and wait. Wait and continue to wait. It's still hot, even hotter than the smaller truck, I didn't think this was possible. My clothes are soaked with sweat and my mouth is so dry that my lips are hard.

Every time I think back to that time I still lose my breath. There was no air, we were crammed. I was suffocating. Reflecting back triggers physical feelings. It was such a challenging experience. Even now while writing this, I'm literally out of breath, sweating, and bizarrely licking my lips!

Mohammed is beside me. My brother. I will do anything for him. I want to protect him. I am all he has and vice versa. I make sure he gets food and water first. Well, I say food, I mean bread. Hard, dry bread and warm water, but it was something. It kept us going.

We then have to change to another lorry. *C'mon, we must be nearly there now,* I think to myself. As we move into the new lorry there is a problem. I hear shouting and screaming. We are climbing onto the new lorry and a police alarm goes off. 'WEE-ow-WEE-ow.' There is panic and chaos. "Run, run, run!" the master shouts. Everyone runs and splits up. "Mohammed!" I cry out, "Mohammed where are you?"

Nothing.

"Brother, brother, can you hear me?"

Frighteningly, still nothing.

I have lost him. I have lost my brother. "Please God, don't do this to me," I whisper!

Mohammed is gone.

What do I do now? Where do I go? He is all I have. What is life without family?

"I'm sorry," I sob out loud. The tears stream down from my eyes. "I'm sorry Mohammed, I have failed you."

Mohammad has either been captured by the police or he made it into another vehicle to travel. I hope and pray it's the latter. I need to believe it is. Do I keep going or go back home? I can't think straight!

Eventually, I compose myself and remember the strength I have and what my family <u>expects</u> of me. OK, I must keep going and inshallah I will meet Mohammed in England.

I have now lost track of the days, weeks maybe. I have grouped with other people from the original truck. I saw them and recognised their faces.

"Hello," I say, "can you help me?"

There and then was the start of my wonderful friendship with Jasur. Thankfully Jasur had some money. He looked after all the costs for the rest of the journey. He is a good man, God will be good to him. We get onto another lorry, and another, and another. We were even on water at one point I think! Thankfully these lorries are not full of other people, so they don't smell as much. They consist of food and big containers. We are told not to touch the food but sometimes we cannot help ourselves, we are starving and we need to survive.

Surviving, this was a challenge. The heat is now not a problem, it is now cold, freezing actually. A temperature I have never experienced. Our lips turn purple and my fingers are numb. How long can we stay like this? Jasur and I have no choice but to hold each other. It has to be done, we need to use each other's body heat to survive.

Out of the blue, the lorry stops. We hear a noise outside. We are shaking, mostly from the cold but also frightened. Then, 'click, clack', 'click' and 'bang'. The door opens. As the daylight shines in, we dip our heads to hide. Have we been caught? Is this the master? The police perhaps? "Go, go, go, out, out, out," we hear. We stand up and jump. We are free.

I look around, I have no idea what time of the day it is but it's grey, very grey and wet. I see factory buildings and many lorries. We did it.

"ALHAMDULILLAH, ALHAMDULILLAH," I cry out loud. We are in England. We have reached the promised land.

"What now?" I ask myself.

Points to consider:

- Do you think that Tariq really wanted to leave his home and family? Was he given a choice? What risks were associated with leaving? What are some of the pros and cons of leaving?

- It is clear that Tariq has a great affection for his family, but was serving them a burden for him?

- Tariq lost his father; how did he respond to this?

- Regarding Mohammed's disappearance, how do you think this may have affected Tariq?

- Tariq has experienced many challenges in this story. At what part of the journey might you have given up?

- How do you think Tariq is feeling emotionally?

What does the CMB Wellbeing Warrior say?

This story demonstrates great courage and resilience. It also displays a major unselfish act from Tariq. We didn't actually hear if Tariq fully wanted to leave or not, in fact, he did suggest that they should all stay together. What was the response to this? All we know is that he was given a great responsibility to look after his brother Mohammed, who unfortunately was abruptly separated from him on the journey.

I do not doubt that this experience was extremely difficult for Tariq, where it could potentially have an impact on how he behaves in the future. When a client comes to me after experiencing a major trauma such as this, I would always refer them to a specialist in this area of work. This is not to say that coaching would not go some way in helping, but we need to appreciate the severity of the situation and how Tariq may be feeling emotionally.

The reality is that Tariq may be grieving from the agony associated with his father's death, Mohammed's disappearance and possibly the dangerous journey he experienced.

We all may grieve for different reasons, such as experiencing a death, a relationship break-up or even moving schools or countries. Research tells us that there are different stages of grief, with a significant emphasis on time. According to the NHS, symptoms of grieving include shock and numbness, lots of crying, tiredness, exhaustion, anger and guilt. If anyone you know is expressing symptoms like this and is grieving, their feelings must be taken very seriously, no matter how you may feel on the matter. These are their feelings, so always try to be present with them in order to support them.

We all experience grief at some point in our lives, and we choose to deal with it in a way that suits us personally. During a coaching session, it is commonplace for a client to want support that is outside the standard coaching model. Sometimes it can be justifiable to adapt the coaching delivery and provide a 'mentoring' style service. Coaching and mentoring are somewhat different in that when coaching, the key is to unearth the natural abilities of the individual, whereas mentoring is when the person delivering the session is more experienced or knowledgeable on the particular area than the client. A mentor will give advice and guidance, a coach won't, or shouldn't anyway if following the correct coaching principles.

In this instance, if a client asks for tips on how to overcome grieving, I would certainly not hold back from providing them with information that will support them. However, in order for the client to understand the difference, I would make it clear that we are moving to a more 'mentoring' style session. We will revisit this later in the book.

Some general ways to deal with grief can be as follows:

- Acknowledge your pain; know you are in the grieving process
- Accept that while grieving, you may experience a range of different emotions
- Take care of yourself physically, this involves diet and exercise
- Seek support from people who care about you
- Participate in your hobbies
- Join a support group
- Get into a good sleeping pattern

Now, getting back to 'coaching', Tariq may come to a session where he demonstrates such grieving symptoms with emotions relating to Mohammed's disappearance and his father's death. In reality, this would be a potential topic. However, for the purpose of this book, let's focus on another possible topic: decision making.

Decision making played a major part in this story, or may have anyway. Let's say that Tariq was asked the following questions: "Do you want to go to England?" and, "Will you take Mohammed with you?"

We don't know the actual answers to these questions, but the reality is that they cannot be easy decisions to make. Imagine that Tariq was indecisive at this point and he needed some clarity over the decision. He knew that unless the justification was clear in his mind, then the outcome could be put into jeopardy.

I get many teenage clients who come to a coaching session with a level of indecisiveness. "Do I want to be here?" "Should I tell the truth?" "What university should I choose?" "Is it time to break up with him/her?" I have heard it all, although I must admit not to the extent of the situation Tariq was put in!

An activity I use when a client expresses a desire to make a clear decision is the *CMB Debate Provoking Paradigm*. In this instance, we explore the decision that needs to be made and look at the *'cost versus benefit'* from a neutral stance. I say neutral, because if there is bias present, the client is then potentially already on the path to making their final decision.

It must be emphasised that when delivering this particular activity, the coach must also demonstrate a neutral stance, and have no personal bias whatsoever towards what they 'think' a client should do. If this is not possible then they are not providing the client with an authentic coaching experience.

After completing this activity with many clients, through using my Co-listening skills (from Chapter 1), I put it to the client what I see. For example, a statement such as, "It seems that you are moving towards option B," will stretch their thinking and challenge them further. I then sit back and see what comes next from them.

Have you heard of the expression 'gut feeling'? From my experience, clients generally go with their gut feeling. Even if the 'cost' list has ten reasons and the 'benefit' list only has five, if you begin to justify the significance of the five, then you have your ultimate answer.

A simple task like this goes a long way to determine the pros and cons of the decision that needs to be made. It opens the door to new possibilities, where a client can get fully behind the decision they were initially unclear about. This sense of clarity will serve the client, as it will eliminate any doubts and enable the individual to proceed with greater confidence and assurance. They can then back themselves moving forward, without any apprehension present.

Enquiry Questions:

Clearly it was a very challenging journey for Tariq. What do you think kept him going? What was his image of England? He used the phrase 'promised land'. What do you think influenced this opinion?

CMB Task:

Have you had to make any decisions recently, or do you have some to make soon? Try the *cost versus benefit* method and see if it supports you. Simply write down the reasons for saying YES to something (benefit) and the reasons for saying NO (cost) and evaluate what you see. In a CMB coaching session we would analyse each one, however today you can be the coach on yourself, try it.

10

Tanisha: Terrorised By Racism

Racism. What's that all about? Does it really happen? Is it something we make up for attention? What racial slurs have I heard? Let's see…Paki, rat, curry muncher, the list goes on. Apparently I am all these things. Hello, my name is Tanisha and I am British. YES, I really am! I was born in England and I have an English accent. Yet, my physical features say otherwise. Here is my painful story.

Firstly, I hope those who tormented me get to read this story. Yes, I'm talking to you: Jane, Omar, Callum and Andrew, I don't forget what you did to me. How could I? You DESTROYED my school experience.

My secondary school life was simply torturous because of the way I looked. I'm not even sure that the word torture gives it justice, I suffered alone so much. Pain like you wouldn't believe. Every day brought a new challenge and generally by the same people.

Being a small-framed kid of Indian descent with big ears didn't help my situation. It gave others ammunition to use against me. I got picked on for looking different from the others in my class. For example, I got called 'Dumbo', because of my large ears, 'rat', because I was small, 'stick', because I was skinny and, worst of all,

'Paki', because of my skin colour. It was something else day after day. They always made me feel like an outcast and I struggled a lot to fit in. Did it really have to be like this just because I'm 'different'?

So let's get this right, I'm Indian, so I get called a 'Paki'…how does that add up? Some people clearly don't know their geography! I suppose this shows the type of people I was dealing with.

What was their problem? Personal anger? Showing off to others? Or maybe they were jealous. Yes, jealousy. *Are they jealous of me?* I would ask myself.

My mum had a good job, so I was lucky that I got to have all the latest gear and go on holidays. These 'other' people, to put it nicely, had a difficult home life, a contrasting one to mine.

I do appreciate that it wasn't easy for them. Their parents were never around. From what I have heard, they came from 'stormy' households that consisted of physical abuse, neglect and had a history of drug and alcohol misuse. Does this make what they did to me OK? I don't think so. I can be empathetic, really I can; I'm a decent person, but to this day, I cannot forgive them. Hate is a strong word, but I do, I still hate them!

Let me take you back on the journey with me. It was a few years ago now. I've since left this particular school; I had no choice. It was either leave or break, and as you will soon see, breaking meant the inevitable. It would have been the end for me!

It all started when I was in Year 8. Year 7 was fine, I had some nice friends and I managed OK. I was surprised with this as I went in expecting the worst. You see, Jane (one of the bullies) was in my primary school and gave me a hard time there. She was nasty, a real monster. I could say much worse about her, but let's just leave it at nasty. Once I heard that she was going to be in the same secondary school as me, I begged my parents to put me in another school.

"Dad, please don't do this to me." "Mum, you know how much she makes my life hell."

But no, they didn't *listen*. They didn't take my claims seriously. If only they had listened to me when I tried to express my concerns, my whole secondary school experience might have been different, in fact, it couldn't have been any worse! Essentially they forced me to go to this school. I never had a chance really, it was evident what the future held for me once they made that decision for me.

I stayed clear of Jane in Year 7. She was in a different form class, so I was out of sight from her most of the time. However, there was one boy in my form class who was very challenging. His name was Omar. He always gave the teacher a hard time and simply dominated the group. He ruined many good lessons and was a thorn in everyone's side. We all just wanted him out. He was intimidating, we were all afraid of him. He was aggressive and, in many cases, filthy, both verbally and physically. He got up to all sorts to the extent that the police were often called. The police even knew him by his first name, which says it all! I stayed clear of him, well, as much as I could.

> But no, they didn't *listen*.

The first day of Year 8 was really the beginning of the end for me in this school. Some form groups had changed. Into my form class came Callum, Andrew and…Jane. I was devastated. These three, along with Omar, formed a 'gang' that was fierce, very fierce.

It started with the usual name-calling and showing off to impress each other. It wasn't just me; the African kids got hit hard too. This was strange, as Omar came from somewhere in Africa. He was the same as me, born in the UK but was a person of colour. He clearly forgot his roots!

One day during class I noticed that my bag had been taken from under my chair. I saw Omar smile at me, which meant one thing. He had not just stolen my bag, but all the contents in it. I found my bag later on, but my wallet and phone were gone. Later that day I found my phone in pieces in the stairwell. I just sat there and cried.

Then there was the bus incident. This was without doubt the lowest point for me. I always left school as soon as the bell rang. I literally ran out the door as fast as I could. I wanted to catch the first bus, the one that's always empty. Well, *usually* empty!

I walked onto the bus and, to my horror, the 'gang' were sitting at the back.

"What?" I said to myself, as my heart began to race.

I then panicked. I was just about to jump off when the door closed in my face. I turned around and sat near the front. At least this way I could jump out when the bus stopped. I felt safer in the front too, as the driver would see if something happened.

As the bus started to drive off, I could see somebody walking down the centre of the bus through the driver's mirror. It was Omar. He came to sit beside me. He sat there for about ten seconds looking at me, staring actually, but said nothing. It was weird, very weird.

He then put his hand on my leg. I was gobsmacked, shaken and in a state of fear. I knew he was dangerous so I had to be smart here. I moved my leg slowly away. He looked at me again and smiled. To this day I can still see his massive, white teeth in my face. It was a smile with a danger underneath, a creepy image. Then he took out a bottle of water, well, that's what I thought it was at first. I looked closer and saw it was yellow in colour and it smelt too. It clearly wasn't water! Disgustingly, he then poured it over my head.

I don't really know how else to describe this other than dirty. I felt so dirty, filthy dirty. As Omar walked to the back of the bus, the others in the 'gang' were laughing at me. I sat there feeling completely exposed in public, horrified at what had just happened. Not one person asked me if I was OK. Was I invisible? Why were these people doing this to me?

I got off the bus as soon as it stopped. I ran in case they were chasing me. I literally ran and ran, without looking back. It was raining, pouring it down. I didn't care, I was wet anyway and this might actually make me feel cleaner. I wanted to tell my parents, but they wouldn't get it, they wouldn't understand, they never did. Somehow they always turned it back on me, saying, "You caused this to happen, so deal with it!" It was always a cold approach from them, with never any empathy toward me and my feelings. It was just so unfair.

It was the same in school when I needed help. I told my school principal about this abuse previously and she brushed me off too. I literally had nobody to turn to. I couldn't see how this would improve. I was in a lonely place, crying out for help, but nobody could see or hear me. What was wrong with me? Could somebody please just acknowledge my pain? Please!

I stopped running and began to walk. I could see a bridge. I climbed up on it and stood there. Looking down the 20ft drop, I could see the train tracks beneath me. The wind and rain were pelting my face. This was painful, but nothing near as painful as what was going on inside me. I was a broken person, emotionally and physically traumatised. I wanted to jump, I really did. I just wanted it all to go away, the pain, constant pain and looking over my shoulder. One thing I do know is that this was not a cry for help; I wanted out. I literally could not continue this way of living any longer. I had two choices, do it and it would be over or endure the abuse. What would you do?

A passer-by, a gentle old man, grabbed me, sat me down and talked me round. He told me that all would be OK, but let's face it, it's not as simple as that. I needed someone to understand me, to see me, to acknowledge what I was going through.

I got home and didn't even tell my parents. It was pointless. I had given up on them understanding me a long time ago. They would find a way to turn it back on me, that it was my fault, the usual.

The next day at school I decided I needed to speak up. I was finally doing it, I'm telling the school principal about these bullies, the whole story. All night I planned this. I was not just doing this for me, but for everyone who this 'gang' bullied. They couldn't get away with this much longer. I was going to use my pain to help others.

OK, here goes. I sat in the principal's office and explained the whole story. I didn't leave anything to chance and went into great detail. In fact, I had written everything down in the middle of the previous night, just so that I wouldn't leave anything out. I presented everything, no stone was unturned. This was an outpour, a real attempt to be heard. My voice. I showed fear, loneliness, sadness and anger, EVERYTHING! I didn't hold back.

My finishing line was, "I'm just broken, please help me!"

Oh, it was such a huge relief to explain how I was feeling. I was so happy with myself for doing it.

The principal looked at me. There was an awkward silence.

"So this happened outside the school building?" she said.

"Yes it did," I responded.

More silence. *I'm not sure I like where this conversation is going*, I thought to myself.

Points to consider:

- What do you think Tanisha is telling us at the end of her story?

- It would be easy for us to think that Tanisha's principal was not supportive. However, we don't know this. What happens if we assume something without knowing the full facts?

- What role did Tanisha's parents play in this story? Was there anything they could have done differently to make sure Tanisha didn't experience what she did?

- What changed when Tanisha took control?

- Did you sense a change in Tanisha's tone near the end of the story?

- How can you tell that the journey to receiving support has begun?

What does the CMB Wellbeing Warrior say?

Anytime a client comes to a coaching session with any mention of suicide, it is crucial to advise them to seek medical help. This is an extremely serious claim from Tanisha, and she will need a professional who deals with this line of work to support her through it. I have no doubt that coaching would help Tanisha, however it is important to recognise and appreciate the significance of such a claim, and make the client aware of the most appropriate services available to them.

Let's begin by looking at the facts. What are the facts here? Firstly, Tanisha was being bullied. Secondly, she didn't feel supported at home by her parents or by the school principal. If we followed the facts from this story, where would a conversation with Tanisha lead? Did you ask yourself why Tanisha's parents and school principal were not supporting her? If you did, please don't!

As Tanisha's coach, we need to tread carefully when using the term 'why'. Asking the wrong question could cause Tanisha to become defensive and may imply that we don't believe her story. In a coaching conversation, if the story is believed or not, we need to hold a neutral perspective and always provide a fair platform for our clients to express what they need to. After all, we must be present to what is being said. This type of conversation can often occur outside of a coaching session. If a friend is ever trying to articulate their feelings to you, try not to ask 'why' and try not to judge. Simply be present.

There is a lot of emotion expressed in this story. It clearly sounds like Tanisha has had a hard time at school. There, it can be as simple as that. Tanisha is longing for visibility and acknowledgement. When coaching, once we acknowledge our client's pain, we are already creating an environment for them to move forward and address their pains further. It's open ground, it's safe. Trust is built.

Have you seen the movie 'Inside Out'? There is a powerful scene where this is demonstrated beautifully. It is when the character 'Joy' confronts another character called 'Bing Bong' when he is upset. She is attempting to cheer him up with her 'joyfulness', but literally has no joy in achieving this. Conversely, when another character called 'Sadness' enters the conversation, something changes. Sadness is fully present in Bing Bong's feelings and demonstrates an understanding of the emotions presented by him. Bing Bong is being met where he needs to be met. There is an acknowledgment between them both. His pain is recognised and compassion is presented by 'Sadness'. This behaviour is what Bing Bong needed in order to feel better, as opposed to somebody pushing him to change his emotions. Check it out, we can all learn a lot from this scene!

Another angle to pursue with Tanisha in a coaching session would be to amplify her actions and the progress that she has made. She sounds proud to speak out in support of others; this is something to celebrate, as it takes great courage to speak out. Can you remember the coaching term from a previous chapter? This is called 'championing'.

A simple statement like, "Tanisha, you are being so brave here," can make her feel at ease.

When there are a lot of emotions presented during a coaching session, I call upon the *CMB Space Invader*, as previously addressed in Chapter 3. However, this time we will also call upon the mythical creature known as the *'Emotional Elephant'*. The *'Emotional Elephant'* is when your behaviour is controlled by how you feel. When our *'Emotional Elephant'* is present, we tend to demonstrate behaviours that are emotionally driven, as opposed to rational and logical. The idea of discussing the *'Emotional Elephant'* during a coaching session is to detach our feelings from our behaviours. This of course is easier said than done!

In this instance, Tanisha can discuss her emotions and explore what triggers them. Could you hear the anger in her story? She is still very angry. This is understandable after all she went through. Ultimately, the bullies destroyed her secondary school life. Statements such as, "I suffered alone so much," "I struggled a lot to fit in," "I cannot forgive them," and, "Hate is a strong word, but I do, I still hate them," are clear indicators that Tanisha is still having difficulties coming to terms with what happened to her.

When we are talking emotionally, we don't always think straight. Emotions are very powerful, and can sometimes stop us from behaving logically or expressing things clearly. They have the potential to get in the way and can be destructive to what we want to achieve. It is possible that Tanisha allowed her emotions to dominate the conversation with her school principal, and therefore didn't get her point across as planned.

When exploring Tanisha's emotions through her 'Emotional Elephant', we can learn more about the behaviours associated with it. Eventually, we learn to step out of the emotional state and into the body of another character called the 'Wise Wizard'. The 'Wise Wizard' thinks differently to the 'Emotional Elephant' and has a tendency to be more trusting when faced with challenges. The 'Wise Wizard' deals with facts, and presents the situation as it appears, without emotional involvement. It takes a no-nonsense approach and has an attitude of 'let's just get on with this'. Picture yourself now, sleeves rolled up and ready to take on whatever is in front of you, that's your 'Wise Wizard'!

With this activity, we change our ways of thinking, from an emotional state to a more logical state. Essentially, we need the 'Wise Wizard' to overpower the 'Emotional Elephant'. This, along with other coaching skills, will go some way to support Tanisha when communicating her feelings to others. In addition, it will help her to move on with her life, with less negative feelings towards this challenging past.

Enquiry Questions:

What do you think the principal's response was? What's making you think this way? What facts do you have to support your point of view? Can you use any of the coaching skills already learned that could potentially change your mindset here? Are you coming to this conclusion emotionally or logically?

eMB Task:

Task 1: Reflect over the last seven days. What emotions did you experience? Did you recognise what triggered such emotions? Ask yourself, "Do I want to feel this way?" If the answer is no, then you need to take control over this. Bring your *'Wise Wizard'* alive, address the trigger and change the way you think about it. Take action!

Task 2: Give yourself a break this week. I'm sure you deserve it! Call a friend and arrange a get-together. Watch the movie 'Inside Out' and see if you can recall the scene I was talking about. Reflect on it afterwards and identify how you can be more like 'Sadness' when a friend is upset.

11

Marco: My Teachers Just Don't Get Me

My name is Marco, and I have all sorts of problems right now. Let's just say my life is difficult, more so than most people my age. I have never met my dad and I am a carer for my mother. I have done this since I was 11, even younger maybe. Home life is hard. I wake up very early and do many duties before leaving for school. I would actually say that being at home is harder than school, school is a break for me! The issue with school is that people make it harder than it needs to be for me. If only they understood me.

My teachers don't get me. They have no idea of the difficulties I have at home. I'm treated the same as everyone else and I don't think it's fair. It's as if I have a loving family, I have money to buy nice stuff and I have the same opportunities as everybody else. Let's be honest here, it's not a level playing field when you compare my situation to others. I get it from teachers all the time: "Marco, why is your homework not done?" "Marco, you missed the deadline," "Marco, why do you not have your letter to go on a trip?"

Well, I'll tell you why Miss, why I don't do my homework, or meet deadlines, or get letters for school trips: BECAUSE I DON'T HAVE HELP AT HOME THE WAY MOST KIDS DO!!

That's right, BECAUSE I don't have parents who will wash my uniform. BECAUSE I have nobody to prepare my lunch. BECAUSE there is nobody available to help me with homework, or help me meet deadlines, or even to sign permission slips for school outings.

BECAUSE, BECAUSE, BECAUSE!

I can give you many examples, if you would just allow me to explain! But no, you just don't *listen*!

The rest of my classmates are so lucky, BECAUSE they get support from home. When I hear the stories of what the other people from my class do at the weekend or on holiday, I get so jealous. It's not even about the latest iPhone or football shirt; it's a clean uniform, a proper PE kit and a packed lunch. The basic things really. This is what I long for, but unfortunately this is all alien to me.

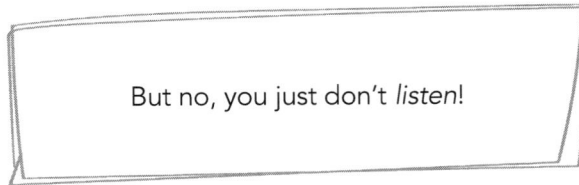

> But no, you just don't *listen*!

Not having stuff like this makes me stand out like a sore thumb. People start to judge me and laugh at me when they see me. For example, I get called names for the poor state of my uniform. It is dirty mostly, and my trousers have holes in them. And as for my teeth, they cause me trouble. I don't have good teeth. My two front teeth stick out and I get abuse for this, it's embarrassing. In fact, would you believe that people have often asked me why I haven't gotten braces yet? What kind of a question is this? It's the same as saying, "You have bad teeth." One statement I have heard many times that really bugs me is, "Why are you so skinny?" I have heard it all. I get called boney, chopsticks, bucky, jaws, pauper, tramp and more!

I mean c'mon, how insensitive is this? OK, I appreciate that I'm not your 'Mr. Handsome' kind of guy, but please don't shove it in my face. It's so hurtful, it really is.

People really need to be more empathetic and sensitive towards how other people feel. Statements and names like these automatically make me feel anxious and insecure about who I am and what I look like. In fact, it makes me not want to talk to people, or laugh, as I'm trying to hide my teeth. As for my weight, yes I am skinny, but I have never really been given good food growing up. We eat what we can afford, usually ready meals from the supermarket or fast food from the local takeaway.

I look at myself in the mirror and see disappointment with regards to the image looking back at me. I compare myself to others and wish I had a different physique. Pale skin, skinny body and bad teeth; life certainly isn't fair! Due to my weight, I go into the toilets to put on my PE kit instead of the changing room. I just don't want other people seeing my body, it makes me uncomfortable and I'm afraid they will laugh. Well, I know they will, it has happened too many times, so my solution is to avoid the situation, get out of their sight and try to be invisible!

Life hasn't been easy for my mum either. My dad left when I was a baby and she was on her own my whole life. It was up to her, and her alone, to look after me and do all the baby work: feeding, changing and washing etc. while getting no sleep! My mum had to do all of this without the presence of her partner or family support. This alone cannot have been easy. I really don't know how she did it. I owe her everything.

To make it more challenging, my mum has a condition. It's progressed over the years and affects her badly now. I won't go into much detail about it, but it means that now I'm looking after her. Our roles have reversed and essentially I have to wash, feed and support her through the day, every day!

We work well as a team, but it feels like it's us against the world. We are doing our best with what we have. We live in a one-bedroom apartment and I sleep on the sofa. Not ideal, but it is what it is, it's the card I have been dealt. I'm not trying to get you to feel sorry for me, and it's certainly not what I want, but I can confidently admit that my life is more challenging than any of the people I go to school with. It's just frustrating that my teachers don't see this.

I do believe that all of this is a test for me. A test where, when I accomplish it, I am ready for the next stage of my life. A life with more opportunities and happier times…I hope! But it's hard. Being at home, looking after my mum in a small apartment, is not the most enjoyable place to be.

I go to school to get away from home life. School is my way out. A way for me to better myself. I want to take this opportunity, as not everyone is offered free education. However sometimes, no, actually many times, I get into trouble. I don't mean to, but things just happen. For example, I'm all about respect. If the teachers don't respect me, then why should I respect them? It's mutual. I am human and they are human, don't speak down to me as if you are better than me…right?

Looking back at my previous years, this attitude has not served me well. It has always caused tension with teachers. Some teachers just didn't get me, they would treat me unfairly and not understand why I didn't have my homework done. "I'm looking after my mother, give me a break!" I have said many times.

One day a teacher was really aggressive towards me. I answered him back, aggressively, probably too aggressively, no, definitely too aggressively! Anyway, the bottom line is that he didn't like it.

"How dare you speak to me like that young man," he says, but I'm thinking, *how dare you speak to me like that...sir!* Then the usual: I get into trouble, detention and another detention.

Remarkably, sometimes I actually like detention. It's time for me just to be left alone in peace. I feel safe here, free from the hounds of emotional abuse from my peers. I sit staring out the window and I think to myself, *what's the point in arguing with the teachers, what do I achieve from it?*

Then the fun starts. I begin to daydream. I like this, it makes me happy. I feel free in my daydreams. I think of movies, football matches or even wonder what life will be like in the future. What kind of job will I have? KFC? NO, the hours are too long, although I would get free food! Becoming a teacher? I don't think so! Why go to school all my life and then choose this as a career? A music artist? Now <u>that</u> I can see myself doing! Anyway, all of these weird thoughts tend to enter my mind when I am in detention. I enjoy doing this. I feel creative and it gives me hope, hope that there is a better life out there for me.

Problems like this with teachers have never left me: arguing, disagreeing and sulking when I don't get my own way. My personal value of respect probably gives me more hassle than it's worth. I ask myself should I change to fit into the system, or does the system have to change for me? Mmmmmm, I know the answer is obvious, but I don't want to admit it!

There is another area that I'm quite embarrassed to talk about: stealing! A lot of the students in school do it. I know people think it's bad, but I look upon it as an opportunity. If someone leaves something behind, like a phone or something, then I believe it's fair game for me to take it. If they are silly enough to lose it, then clearly they don't care enough about it. Also, if I get something and sell it, I will have money to buy food and more stuff for home. For example, last month I found a wallet. I looked around to see who lost it. Honestly, I would have given it back, but nobody admitted to owning it, so it was either leave it back on the floor for somebody else to take, or keep hold of it and support my mum. I did the latter and bought a new kettle for the house. We needed a new one badly, so you can decide if this is a good or bad way to go about it. It's every man for himself, dog eat dog in the circles I'm in!

However, things like this have caused me trouble in school and also outside of school with the police. As I said, everybody does it and I feel as if I don't have a choice. I need to survive. I am hoping to get away from these circles, but at the moment I don't see a way out. I could tell you many stories about the people I know and hang out with, but I don't think they are appropriate for this platform. Dark stories, real dark, you really wouldn't believe them, they would shock you!

One good thing I would like to say about school is that I have discovered many sports. Cycling is something I really enjoy doing. It's not on the curriculum, but when my teacher Mr. Davies found out that I could not cycle, he arranged for the police to give me an unclaimed stolen bike. He stayed behind every Thursday for a few months to teach me how to cycle. Ever since then I now cycle to school and to the shops. In fact, I cycle everywhere I go, or at least everywhere I can. It was such a great life skill to learn. I wish school was more about life skills such as this.

Ironically my bicycle got stolen. I suppose I can't complain, what goes around comes around…I think that's the saying anyway! But, thankfully, I now have a new bike, a lovely red bike and importantly this time a chain lock to go with it, so hands off!

When I think back to when Mr. Davies was teaching me how to cycle, it made me think about all the wonderful things my teachers did to support me at school. At the start of the story, I did say that teachers didn't get me, didn't understand me, and treated me unfairly. In reality, these statements are wrong. This is me playing the victim. I was the one being difficult. I think now that I am that little bit older, I can look back with a different perspective. A perspective that is not about me the victim, but me the person. Yes, I have empathy towards myself and I do understand why I was so difficult with regards to teachers not respecting me, but I also understand that I need to give respect in order to receive respect. If school has taught me anything in preparation for the real world, it's to show off the best of me in every opportunity. This includes the skills of accepting, communicating 'effectively' (not just my way) and appreciating others and how they feel. I regret being disrespectful, I regret stealing, but I cannot change the past. It's time to move on and use the experiences as a learning curve. It's time to be a better me, this is what will help me most in life. Wish me luck!

Points to consider:

- What did you notice about Marco's attitude at the end compared to the beginning of the story?

- Marco used the word victim; does he have the right to play the victim role here?

- Life clearly is not easy for Marco and he has expressed this deeply, however, can you identify any point in the story where he is making things more difficult for himself?

- Is there anything Marco could have done differently?

- What key learning took place?

- Marco mentioned that 'everybody does it', when referring to stealing. Does this justify his actions? What would happen if we all followed what others do?

What does the CMB Wellbeing Warrior say?

Firstly, I would like to say well done to Marco for many things. The role he plays as his mother's carer cannot be easy for any young person. He clearly has a great sense of love and kindness towards his mother, which is commendable. What would be possible if we all demonstrated this behaviour towards our parents? How do you think they would feel? What effect would this have on the relationship between you and them?

Secondly, I would like to acknowledge Marco for his use of reflection skills. Reflection is such a powerful tool. A personal reflection model I use is that from David Kolb's 'Experiential

Learning Cycle'. Experiential learning simply means learning from our experiences through reflecting, planning and doing. In Marco's story, he indirectly demonstrates the use of this model when he sees that his attitude was wrong, and that he needed to change this in order to get a different outcome. A quote often attributed to Albert Einstein follows a similar approach: 'Insanity is doing the same thing over and over and expecting different results.' Of course, I'm not suggesting for one minute here that Marco is becoming insane, but he clearly used this method of thinking to change his attitude to obtain a different outcome. Can you see the similarities?

Can you envisage what the future would hold for Marco if he did not change this attitude? I can only imagine that he would have become more and more frustrated in school each day, and this would lead to a very negative spiral. This is something I have seen first-hand during my teaching career and, unfortunately, it is not a good place to be in. School is not easy, and with so many demands you need everybody around you to be on your side. School is a team effort, where students, parents and teachers need to work cohesively in order to be successful!

Marco mentioned the word 'victim'. This is a powerful word and would be an area to explore further. As expressed earlier, I completely empathise with him on how challenging his life must have been. The troubles he has experienced with comments about his body and teeth can only portray a negative image of the people around him. However, if this was a coaching session, it would be important to get the client to step out of this self-pity place and into a headspace that involves more self-empowerment. Everybody has a choice on how to think and behave. We either choose to be upset about something, or we choose to get over whatever it is that is upsetting us. As previously seen with the fictionalised characters of the *'Emotional Elephant'* and the *'Wise Wizard'*, there can be more than one personality type within us, so essentially we need to decide which personality we are feeding. Keep reminding yourself that you always have a choice!

In this instance, is Marco feeding his energy to the *'Wise Wizard'* or the *'Emotional Elephant'*? A good question here would be: "Marco, who are you being right now and what are the feelings associated with being this person?" What do you think the next question should be?

We will now focus on how to further support Marco in a coaching session. As always, there are many ways to achieve this, and each individual coach will have their own unique method. I could sense a theme of fairness and victimisation throughout the story. This can provide a good platform to know where to start and what approach would serve Marco best. Can you recall any coaching tools that could be applied here?

It would be a good time to apply the *CMB Proven Truth Tactic*. For example, if one of Marco's 'truths' (as referred to in Chapter 7) was that 'life is fair', then he has every reason to feel victimised, and wake up every morning angry and frustrated, as clearly he feels that his life is not fair. Alternatively, if Marco held a view that one of his 'truths' was that 'life is not fair', then he can come to accept the injustice and challenges that he is faced with and move on. This is not as easy as it sounds, and it undoubtedly takes time to develop a mindset like this.

Another avenue to empower Marco here is to use something called his *'Inner Leader'*. It is very common for us all to dissect our failures, so let's do the same with our successes. In a coaching session, I refer to this as the *CMB Authoritative Content Commander*. For this, we conduct a series of exercises to unveil who Marco's unique *'Inner Leader'* is and what personality characteristics it possesses. To put it simply, your *'Inner Leader'* is you at your best, the 'you' who needs to turn up in order to get the results you desire. The 'you' who needs feeding, to tackle the challenge in front of you.

For example, we all have self-doubt about something, especially when making tough decisions. When I experience this, I focus on my own 'Inner Leader' and let its personality take over and deal with the situation. Your 'Inner Leader' is YOU, just a more authoritative you!

The desired result here is that by using his 'Inner Leader', Marco will put himself in an assertive place, where he has better capabilities to deal with whatever is put in front of him.

Enquiry Questions:

What do you think is the key message that Marco is trying to express through his story? What is his biggest challenge?

CMB Task:

Close your eyes and reflect on a time when you performed at your best. Fully embrace yourself in that moment. Think about the environment, the sounds, the people involved and the smells etc. What did you do to make this moment successful? What skills did you demonstrate on this day? What were your personality traits? Grab a pen and paper and write them down.

Repeat this using different successful experiences and continue to write down the personality traits that made these moments successful. Eventually, you will join the dots and create your unique 'Inner Leader'. Now, give it a name and call upon it when needed.

12

Daniel: Dealing With My 'Disability'

When I was younger and had just moved to a new school, there was a point where I was getting bullied very badly due to the fact that I had a disability. My disability was that I couldn't talk properly: I had a stammer. Now when I say bullied, I'm not talking about being kicked or punched. I'm talking about comments, staring and social media harassment. It is very unkind and impossible to get away from it. Due to social media, it's 24/7!

I don't stammer all the time, only when I get nervous. But let's face it, children can be ruthless, insensitive and vulgar, so once found out, there was no hiding place for me in this barbaric environment. I am Daniel and this is my story.

It all started in an English lesson on the first day. The teacher, who doesn't know me properly yet, asks me a question, and…BOOM. Here it goes. Just when I don't want 'it' to let me down, it happens. I freeze. I cannot get anything out of my mouth. I'm trying, I really am, but my physical body just won't respond to what my brain wants it to do. People are staring. The teacher doesn't realise what the issue is, as he saw me speak earlier, albeit when I wasn't nervous!

He waits for my answer, and continues to wait. I physically cannot do it. I want to, but I can't. I can feel my face go red. Sweat on my forehead. My whole mouth feels numb. My head is literally about to explode. It's like one of those dreams where you feel you are trying to talk but your mouth literally wont open, like it's stitched together or something. I want my body to do something, but it's not reacting.

One boy laughs. And then another and another. Everybody is now laughing or sniggering at me. The teacher has lost control of the class, it's a big joke and I am that joke, me and my stammer!

That evening my friend John messaged me. He asked if I had seen what was posted on social media. I hadn't, I was afraid to go on it in case somebody had put something up about me regarding today's incident. Regrettably for me, they did. John told me that I wouldn't like it if I saw it, so advised me not to look. What would you do? What I don't see won't hurt me…right? C'mon, who am I kidding? I needed to see!

As I lift the phone to check it, my hands are shaking. My face is boiling and I am feeling extremely anxious. I have the heartbeat of a person about to do a bungee jump. Then, right there on screen, I see it. Humiliation doesn't represent how I feel, I need a word that is worse than that. It's a picture of a donkey but with my face. 'DONKEY DANIEL' the headline says.

The whole school is laughing at me. How can I go to school tomorrow? I sit on my bed and cry. Why do people have to be so cruel? I can't help my stammer. It's not as if they are perfect themselves. What is their objective? Is it to demotivate me and make me feel as though I am not the same as everyone else? If that is the case they have succeeded, they have won. I am defeated, congratulations!

I want to talk to somebody about how I am feeling, but my parents are never around and my nanny, although amazing at so many things, wouldn't know how to deal with this. My best friend? Well, his response is always positive. Too positive in fact, in an unsupportive sort of way. I can picture him now if I was to express how I feel. He would say, "Ah, don't worry, it will be OK, it will blow over."

But will it? How does he know? He doesn't know my pain. He can't feel my chest, my pounding heartbeat and the strain coming from it. So no, I don't tell him how I feel, he just won't get it. It's me and me alone, as usual. I literally have nobody who will *listen* to me.

The next morning comes around after a night of torture that consisted of no sleep and negative thoughts of how the school day will go. My heart was constantly racing and I simply couldn't relax. Tossing, turning and sweating, lots of sweating, it was horrendous.

Breakfast? No thanks! I cannot eat, I feel empty, sick actually. I go to school and sit quietly. Complete paranoia. Is everyone looking at me? What are they saying about me? A few lessons go by and nothing has been said. Is it over? Please let it be!

> I literally have nobody who will *listen* to me

Unfortunately for me, it isn't.

Lunchtime comes, and a boy who thinks he is funny shouts at me, "Hey donkey, donkey Daniel!" Everyone laughs. I want to respond but physically can't. I'm nervous and angry. Not a good combination for anyone with a stammer!

This became a long-standing joke, donkey this and donkey that. Externally I can laugh it off, but deep down I'm not laughing. I'm pretending that I'm OK with it. Of course I'm not, but I'm trying not to show them that they are hurting me. What else can I do? Any suggestions?

Another thing I have done to help me through this is to avoid people. I don't get into conversations and I don't get involved in class discussions. I have been getting outside help and I am improving. But talking with a doctor, or communicating at home with my family, is a different setting from school. It's just not the same.

I feel like the donkey situation has scarred me for life. If only they knew what they were doing to me. It has given me an anxiety problem about school, and how people judge me. I could be sitting on the sofa watching TV and when I think of school I immediately get a physical sensation throughout my body. Not a good sensation, but a nervous feeling. Have you ever experienced this? I hope you haven't, it's not nice. I wouldn't wish it on anyone.

School is like a negative trigger for me. One minute I'm fine, and then I think of school and BANG. Pain all through my body. I wish the people who did this could experience my suffering. I often wonder if they have their own worries? I see so many people having a great time at school, and I think to myself, *I wish I was more like that, they don't have a worry in the world, they are happy.*

During these difficult times at school, I find myself thinking a lot. It's lonely for me. When I'm with my friend I am OK, but he is not with me in every lesson. I have other friends, quiet boys too. I never wanted to hang out with the so called 'cool' people. In fact, I despise what they stand for. It's like, "Hey look at me!" and, "I am funny, laugh at what I do!"

It's pathetic really. I find it childish, but it seems that anyone who goes against the grain with them is not accepted into their circles. They are controlling, dominant, and they want all the girls to like them. I actually think that the girls find them immature, to be perfectly honest.

The really hurtful thing is that some of the boys in this group were my friends in primary school. They've just jumped ship to be 'in with the gang'. When I see them on their own separately, they are actually nice and pleasant to me. However, when the pack is together they are show-offs, bullies, horrible boys.

I used to live in the same area as one of them. When I saw him at home in our community we would talk and all would be fine between us, but when in school he was a completely different person. It was like this group possessed him, made him not so pleasant, an evil version of his true self.

Every day they all hang out. I walk by them in the corridor nervously, smile, whilst deep down I'm praying that they won't turn on me. Sometimes they don't, but most times they do. Donkey noises are the predictable taunts!

I am adamant not to feed them and give them the attention that they want. Yes, I would like to react, but I stay quiet. I have decided that the best thing to do is to ignore them and let them say whatever they want, as I have learned not to care.

After some time, they are starting to say less stuff. It is like, if I stay quiet, I'm off their radar. Unfortunately, this is not good news for somebody else! There is more prey out there to hunt, more unfortunate victims.

This is where I am today with it all. I'm happy to be off their radar, happy to pass the time being invisible. I suppose you could say I'm an in-betweener, just like the TV show, but in a different way, a way that suits me, a way where I can get through the school day without getting the p**s taken out of me and without having to speak to many people. Yes, it can be hard, lonely actually, but that's me and that is my school life. Would you want it?

Points to consider:

- What would you like to say to Daniel right now?

- Did you get a sense that he has given up on himself?

- Daniel mentioned that the boys in 'the gang' didn't have a worry in the world; does he know this for sure? Where is the evidence?

- Is Daniel comparing his life to others, and if so, will this help him?

- Daniel mentioned that he was 'alone as usual' - where do you think his parents are? Could Daniel ask them for help?

- If the boys at school knew how Daniel was feeling, do you think they would continue to give him a hard time? What can Daniel do to make them aware of how he feels?

What does the CMB Wellbeing Warrior say?

Regrettably, I have had the experience of dealing with a story like this all too often. I can sense that Daniel has given up on himself. Once we accept this from ourselves, it is very hard to climb out of this dark hole. Daniel used the expressions 'avoiding people' and 'learning not to care'. As a coach, seeing this type of behaviour is alarming and, if a client demonstrates such traits, I would be eager to change their mindset to one that can offer more positive opportunities.

We briefly touched on the 'avoiding tactic' earlier in Chapter 8 with Jo. This really isn't the long term answer to Daniel's problems. What does the future hold for Daniel when he is behaving like this?

In a coaching session I refer to this as the *'Delaying Dodger'*. The objective here is to make the client aware that turning a blind eye really isn't the solution, and another approach would offer better future prospects. Essentially, we need to delve deeper and cultivate Daniel's skills, so that he is able to deal with the challenges he is experiencing, as opposed to running away from them. Once awareness is attained, with regards to the bypassing of a situation, Daniel can then begin to put the building blocks in place to tackle such challenges with a new approach.

It also sounds like Daniel needs an injection of self-worth, a sense of belief and drive for him to feel that he has much more to offer in his life. Sometimes as a coach, we need to take control and be firm with our client. A coach will know what will work for their clients and, therefore, should be able to gauge if this method is appropriate or not. Some clients like a soft, sensitive approach and others like the 'no filter just say it' way of doing things. It is worth pointing out that this can be dangerous territory for a coach, as it can lead to a more mentoring conversation.

As explained earlier, coaching and mentoring are noticeably different, and there are times when a client might request a more 'mentoring style' approach from their coach. Again, this is OK, providing the coach explains this to their client. For example, in this instance I would say, "I'm now taking off my coaching hat," to classify such distinctions.

Asking Daniel some powerful questions in this instance, where he might experience some cognitive challenge, can go some way towards making him feel different about the situation. Daniel will soon come to terms with the fact that he needs to stop accepting things the way they are, and start taking control himself. Eventually, there will be a realisation that, "YES, I do have more to give, I AM better than this, I WON'T tolerate this behaviour anymore."

Now, I'm not suggesting that Daniel storms over to these boys and gives them a taste of what he is feeling, but, through empowering Daniel with more positive methods of thinking, he will be in a better position to deal with his challenges.

One method of instilling self-belief in people is to apply the use of affirmations. Have you ever tried this? It is a very simple yet powerful way of helping you adjust your subconscious thoughts, gaining self-belief, rewiring your way of thinking and embracing change. When doing this, we are essentially helping Daniel to develop his negative behaviours into more positive ones. The key here is to add significant positives to Daniel's life, where we look at his basic needs and explore what has to happen in order to add increased value to his life.

In a coaching session, this is achieved during the *CMB Firm Declaration Formula* and will go some way in helping Daniel to live a better life and achieve greater success from simply thinking positively. It supports the development of a *'growth mindset'* and aids change.

There are many ways to perform affirmations. For example, closing your eyes and visualising them, recording a voice memo on your phone and listening back to them, or simply writing them down on scraps of paper and placing them where you can see them easily, such as on your bathroom mirror or fridge.

Affirmations usually begin with, 'I can, I am, I know, I love'. However, this is not a concrete rule.

In Daniel's case, here are some possible examples of affirmations he could use:

- I am strong and healthy
- I can be who I want to be
- I am proud of who I am
- I give myself permission to achieve better things
- I have the confidence to talk to people
- I love myself no matter what
- I treat myself with kindness and respect
- All my relationships are meaningful and fulfilling
- Today I am open to opportunity
- Today I am willing to fail in order to succeed
- Today my own wellbeing is my priority

Regarding adding value to Daniel's basic needs here, a good place to start is by knowing exactly what makes him happy. Once he knows this, he can simply add value by allowing more of this into his life. A strategy such as this is something you can implement in your own life. Conversely however, the opposite can be said for what makes you sad. In simple terms, add more of what makes you happy and eliminate what makes you sad as much as you can. This, along with the use of affirmations, will go some way into becoming a more happy, positive person, which in turn will make you a more 'attractive' person to be friends with. Now, when I say 'attractive', I don't mean in beauty terms, I mean attracting the right people towards you. By being more attractive, you are opening up more possibilities and opportunities, as you are now more approachable and likeable.

Enquiry Questions:

Is there anybody like Daniel in your life? Explore and reflect to see if you know of anybody who you or your peers may laugh at and think it's OK, because they are OK with it. Are they really OK with it? How could you find out? What could you do if you were to find out that you have been hurting them all this time?

eMB Task:

Task 1: Create your own affirmations! Make a list of priorities in your life that you would like to focus on. Decide how you would like to conduct your affirmations and go for it, stretch yourself and see what is possible.

Task 2: Devise a list of what makes you happy and what makes you sad. What can you do with this list? If unsure, refer to the response to Daniel's story!

13

Fatima: I Just Don't Fit In

Hello. My name is Fatima. When I answered these questions about my school experience it really got me thinking. Do I like it? Erm, yes, I do now. But before, things were different, very different actually. I despised school to be honest. School was like a stone in my shoe, a disturbing part of my life that just wouldn't go away. Day in and day out, this stone just kept getting sharper and sharper and cutting deeper and deeper!

Regarding my feelings now, school is great. My teachers are wonderful and I love my friends, I really do. They know me, we trust each other and have each other's backs all the time. I always look forward to break time to see them and we hang out together. In fact, we do everything together. They get me and I get them. We are not the 'cool' girls or anything, far from it; but we are who we are, and if people don't like us, they can just leave us alone!

I sound like a strong-minded person right? I am, and I'm proud of this. I have come a long way. My journey into believing in myself and not caring what other people think took a lot of work, a lot of help and unfortunately a lot of pain, real pain. A word of warning, you may find my story distressing!

Let me take you back to the start. I have had to move schools many times. This was because my dad's job kept changing locations. I would start in one school, build relationships and then we were on the move again. The development of friendships was never easy for me. To be honest, I'm not the most open with people. I've been hurt by 'friends' in the past, so I am careful with who I let into my life. Too many of them ended up being fake and making up stuff. They did whatever it took to fit in. I got fed up with how it made me feel, sick of them trying to be people they are not. I don't want to change who I am just to fit in. Also, as we move home regularly, I find that sometimes I'm just not bothering to make new friends. I find it's energy-sapping, and in the end the friends I make end up drifting away when I move, even if we promise not to let this happen! Do you know what I mean?

OK, I must admit that it's not always a choice for me. I didn't have people queuing up wanting to be friends with me. I'm big for a girl, big-boned I like to say. Others would describe me differently, unpleasantly differently.

It all started in primary school. I noticed that I was getting bigger than the other girls. I observed that I was physically developing faster than my classmates. I would be as good as the boys in PE, and I was more interested in hanging out with them, more so than the girls. I just felt I could relate to the boys better.

As I moved into secondary school, I noticed that my arms and legs were well-toned. I suppose you could say I'm quite 'masculine'. I have short hair and I do accept that I don't look like your 'girly type' of girl, if that makes sense! I'm OK with this. It's the body I have been given. But again, looking back to previous years, I wasn't always so strong minded about this.

I play a lot of basketball, and have done so for as long as I can remember. I have always been the school captain and it was on the court where I felt at complete ease, safe and happy overall. I felt protected on the court. Nobody could hurt me there. I was good and I knew I was good. The coach was great and she used my strengths to benefit the team. The girls on the team were great too (well, most of them). On the court, playing basketball was me at my best.

However, during this time, my physical characteristics caused me problems. People would call me a boy or a lesbian. Lesbian, always lesbian actually. I'm not a lesbian, but what if I was? What was the problem? If that's what people are then fine, leave them to it, let them be happy!

One day, I was in class and we were watching a video about a woman in the Olympics, a physically strong woman. The objective of this video was to empower people, girls in particular, to use their body types to their advantage. Because this woman was muscular, she competed in the shot put event. Her name was Natalya and she was the world record holder. However, due to her muscular, athletic body, people started laughing, as she was somewhat different to your 'normal-bodied' woman, if there is such a thing!

Some people in the class started to look towards me and snigger. They started calling me Natalya. Why? I don't know. My hair? My big-boned body? My success in sports? I asked them to stop, but they just wouldn't *listen*! Whatever the reason, it wasn't nice.

That day during lunchtime, a group of girls began to call me Natalya. To make it more hurtful, one of these girls was on my basketball team. On the team she was lovely to me, but outside, just because she was with her 'gang', she was not so nice. These girls were pathetic anyway, always wanting the attention of the boys and wearing clothes that would grab attention, clothes that I knew their parents would not approve of. They would leave the house in an outfit and then change before hanging out. Oh, you wouldn't believe what they got up to outside of school with boys, but I'd better not say. I even saw 'stuff' going on in school, stuff that I could tell they were doing for approval, just for the boys to like them and to be popular. They clearly had no respect for themselves!

Being a teenager in today's society is difficult. The expectation, the fitting in, the not going against the grain and the 'just do it' attitude, just do what everybody else is doing. No, not for me, thank you. It's stuff I wouldn't do as I have too much respect for myself. What's wrong with being different? What's wrong with attempting to follow my own path, doing things my own way?

> I asked them to stop, but they just wouldn't *listen*!

Unfortunately, this attitude didn't always serve me too well. I consciously didn't want to be like everybody else, so I did 'my thing'. I would play sports, I'd hang out with whoever I felt was nice, not because they were popular, but simply because they showed kindness and respect towards me. Sometimes it was boys, sometimes it was girls, essentially it was whoever made me feel happy. Outside of school, I wore clothes that I wanted to wear, not because they were fashionable, but because I was comfortable in them. This was me, like it or not.

Due to the way I did things and because of how I looked, many girls made my school days very difficult. Constant name-calling, lesbo, lezzer and Miss Butch, for example. I heard them all. It wasn't nice, it really wasn't.

Eventually it took control of me, it got the better of me. I began to lose the strength and character I used to have. I had lost my identity and I simply lost belief in myself. I was experiencing paranoia because of all this constant judgement people were showing towards me. I wanted it to end, I honestly did. It got to a stage where I could see no way out. I wanted to end my life.

Shamefully, I used to have images in my mind about suicide, like seeing myself hanging from a tree. I'm not sure why; I must have seen it in a movie or something. I certainly wasn't proud of it. But, I couldn't do it, could I?

One day, I was home alone in the kitchen. I was in so much pain, emotional pain. I despised how I was being treated by others. I had lost faith in what the human race represented, as too often I was getting picked on for the way I looked. Why did it have to be like this?

My body and how it appears to others is causing this pain. I now had a hatred towards it, a separation between my mind and my body. I viewed it with shame. I picked out a knife from a drawer.

This is all your fault, you are my enemy. Why make my life so difficult? I'm going to do it, I'm going to hurt you.

This was a strange psychological situation, where I was detaching my body from me, the person. Weird, right? But, remember I was not in a good place, so please don't judge me for this. I was hurting and the pain wasn't going away. Every name, every snigger towards me, would feed this person inside me, a person who had venom towards their own body. Who was I becoming? This wasn't me... was it?

I stood in front of a mirror, tears streaming down my face. I looked at the knife. I wanted to do something, but I didn't know what. I wasn't sure of what outcome I wanted. I asked myself:

Do I really want my life to end, or do I just want to hurt this body? What if I hurt myself and survive? I will be scarred forever. But if I do do this, will everybody who called me names now stop? Yes, this is the best outcome. If everybody stops calling me names then I can be happy. I won't have to deal with this constant torture every day. Yes, a cry for help, this is what this is. I don't really want to die!

OK, so here goes. I hold the knife up, I slide my finger along the blade, to feel its sharpness. It feels blunt...is this good? No, possibly not. But, I do it. I run the blade across my wrist, attempting to draw blood. But sure enough, the knife is too blunt, and I can't break the skin. *Christ*, I think, *I'm gonna have to saw!*

I then started to see people, the people who make my life not worth living. I could hear the name-calling, "BOY, LESBIAN, NATALYA," and the rest.

I cried, I was in pain, physically and mentally. Trust me, this was not nice. I began to lose control of my body. It was like I was on the outside looking in, sawing and watching my arms turning bloodier and bloodier. And then...

I stopped.

Out of the blue, I just felt a strange, ghostly sensation. It was like a voice in my head, or a family member in heaven just took the knife from my hand and hugged me. Honestly, it's hard to explain, but I went from acting crazily to a sense of complete calmness in the space of seconds. It was like an out-of-body experience, it really was. Everything seemed as if it was in slow motion. I could breathe again, I was unrecognisably calm.

I took this as a sign. I stopped hurting myself there and then. I washed the blood off and put the knife back. I sat thinking. The monster was now gone. It was out of me. I was safe. My mind and body were connected again.

Whatever it was, or whoever it was, helped me, it worked. Somebody was looking out for me, somebody cared for me. "Thank you," I said as I looked up to the ceiling with a completely changed state of mind.

Ever since that day, I have changed my perspective of my body. I now use it as a resource. I use it to make myself better. I'm not ashamed of it. I embrace it. I want to maximise my opportunities and, if my body can do anything to help, then great.

I look at it as a tool. Maybe a career in professional sport? Maybe a career in sport in general. Anyway, I continue to play basketball and other sports. This has made me gain new friends; proper friends, not fake ones. Friends who share the same interests as me, who are attracted to the same things I am. I'm so relieved, I spend my time with people I can share conversations with, people I don't need to argue with, people who like me. Yes, as simple as that. People who like me for who I am!

As I said at the start, I'm strong now, mentally. Many of my friends are boys and I'm OK with that. They are good people and they care for me. When I get called names I can deal with it. I think back to that surreal moment with the knife and remember the calmness that came with it. Someone out there is protecting me, and you know what, I don't know who you are, but thank you. You saved my life and I won't let you down. I also won't let myself down either, me and my body, together as one.

Points to consider:

- What do you think happened to Fatima emotionally when she was cutting herself?

- Fatima expressed that 'someone' is looking out for her; what are your thoughts on this?

- It sounded like Fatima started off as a very strong character. However, according to the story, this eventually caused her problems and did not serve her too well. Why do you think this was the case?

- What changed in Fatima's personality in order for her perspective to change?

- Fatima said that she now uses her body as a resource; what do you think she means by this?

- What message can you take from Fatima's story?

What does the CMB Wellbeing Warrior say?

As always, when I hear any mention of suicide, I would be advising Fatima to see a medical professional. As coaches, it is important to be honest with our client and make clear distinctions between what we can achieve, and what we cannot. We must always put the client's health first and never make false claims, so in this instance, a referral would be advised. However, as previously stated, coaching can still add great value, as it can coincide with other support that a client may be receiving.

It was evident from Fatima's story how courageous she was at the beginning. It was lovely to hear such powerful phrases used, such as: "I don't want to change who I am just to fit in," and, "What's wrong with attempting to follow my own path?" Unfortunately, this tone changes as the story progresses, and it was clear that the distasteful girls really affected the type of person that Fatima became, and how she viewed her body.

In a coaching session, we already have a wonderful resource to call upon here. Do you know what it is?

It's Fatima and her old ways of thinking and behaving. Like in previous chapters, we can explore the skills and traits Fatima possesses when she is being her best. We can see who she has now become as a result of a change in behaviour, and then contrast and compare outcomes. This simple yet effective activity can support an individual when they are not performing at their best. Sometimes, a client just needs a reminder of what they are capable of and what resources they have at their disposal.

At this point, I would like to focus Fatima's energy on her U-turn at the end of the story. I have to 'champion' Fatima here; the way she reframed her feelings about her body, from disliking it to using it as a tool to support her in life, was admirable. Can you recall this from Chapter 4? I used this as a tool for Alfie, where it supported his mindset on his own body, his 'skinny' legs to be precise.

The reality here is that Fatima ended up coaching herself. She bravely changed her perspective and looked at her body with a newfound appreciation. Her words were so powerful: "I now use it as a resource," "I use it to make me better," "I'm not ashamed of it," "I embrace it," "I want to maximise my opportunities and if my body can do anything to help, then great," and "I look at it as a tool."

Statements such as this sound somewhat like affirmations, and clearly there is a transformation taking place here. Fatima is now in control, she is directing her energy to a good place; she is embracing change! Fatima now looks at her body as an opportunity, an opportunity for career prospects. She has simplified her way of thinking and expressed, "OK, this is what I have been given, what can I achieve with it?" With an attitude like this, the possibilities are endless for Fatima.

When I get a 'coach-like' client such as Fatima, I would acknowledge that she has in fact coached herself. I would further empower her to have the confidence to continue to do so. Yes, there are many coaching tools that she can learn in a coaching session, but she has a wonderful sense of self-awareness, resilience and commitment to herself, a cocktail of skills that will lead Fatima to potential greatness.

Enquiry Questions:

What if Fatima was describing this 'out-of-body experience' to you, but you had different beliefs or thought processes on the matter; is it worth telling her what you believe, or is it best to allow her to portray this in her own way? What would the outcome be if you expressed an opinion that challenged hers?

eMB Task:

Look at your body. Explore its characteristics. Is it long and slim? Short and wide? Or somewhere in-between? In scientific terms, we refer to these as 'somatotypes'. Your somatotype describes the type of body shape and physique you have. If you can, do some research on this and explore which somatotype you possess, and see what sports or recreational activities would suit your body best. You have one body, maximise its potential! Coach yourself, just like Fatima did!

14

Daria: My 'Disorder'

ello. I'm Daria and I have ADHD. There, I have said it. This is probably the way I should introduce myself to people. What do you think? Straight to the point or too blunt? Well, from my experience it could make things easier for me by saying it like this!

ADHD stands for 'Attention Deficit Hyperactivity Disorder', which basically means I can't concentrate on one thing, because my brain thinks I need to do everything at once. That's how I describe it anyway! A good analogy for it is that all brains have a door, so in a 'normal' person's brain, the door opens and information goes in, and the door closes so the information can't come out. However in my brain, the door is always open, therefore information doesn't stay in my head. This is frustrating, especially at school when I am trying to learn things.

From my experience in school, the teachers and students were not very understanding or supportive of my disorder. One particular teacher, Miss Baker, really made my life very difficult.

I am a very bubbly girl and feel that I have a likeable personality. One day in class I was just being my normal self and showing the happy side of me when things got out of hand. It was the last day of the school week and, OK, maybe I was slightly over-excited for the weekend to come, but because of my overly happy behaviour, my teacher asked me if I had my medication. She said this in front of the whole class. I was quite shocked by this. It offended me greatly, as not everyone was aware of my condition. Everybody was looking at me and some people started to snigger. I wanted the floor to eat me up, I really did. My friend who I was talking to was looking at me in pity, as if to say, "Oh no, this is sooooooooooo embarrassing for her."

I felt like this was an attack on me, like the teacher was jealous of my happiness that particular day. Miss Baker is not a nice person; think of Cruella de Vil from 101 Dalmatians and you will have a good idea of her personality! I disliked Miss Baker so much that I even used to sit and eat my lunch slowly, just so that I would be late to her lesson, therefore minimising the amount of time I had to spend with her. Honestly, it was that bad!

Before each lesson I always had a pain in my chest. In fact, the whole morning when I would think about this particular lesson, the pain would rise up through my chest, just like a headache. Everything would be good and normal, and then my brain reminded me of this lesson and…there it would be again, the pain.

Sorry, I got distracted there, now, back to the story…! I do this a lot you see, I get easily distracted. When I'm doing something and I think of something else, I…AHHHHHHHH, I've just done it again. Sorry!

Sooooooooo, back to the story (again!). I simply responded with, "Yes, I have my medication," in a low, distinctively sad voice. As I sat at my desk, I felt so victimised. I felt like everyone was looking at me, like I had some sort of disease. After the lesson I ran and locked myself in the toilets. The windows were open and it was freezing. I just stood there crying in silence, alone in the cold, with a horrible drain water smell. It was so cold that I could see my breath!

The tears were running down my face, and even they were cold! I felt like I could not breathe and I was swearing out loud and punching the walls. I needed out, I hated this place. I didn't know what to do. I looked at myself in the mirror. I saw pity, anger and disappointment. Why me? Why did I have to have this 'illness'? It was just not fair.

Thankfully, I had a lovely, understanding teaching assistant. She came to get me. I explained to her how I felt, so she reassured me that I didn't have to go back to class that day. She said I could go and sit in the library and help the librarian. This is where I felt happy. I was with people who understood me and who were nice to me. How come I felt so much more comfortable with adults? I was only 14 but preferred being in the company of adults, do you know what I mean? I wished I could stay there all day every day, but unfortunately, I knew I couldn't. The next morning it was back to school as normal. Oh how I hated that place.

On another day, I experienced this again, only this time with students. Why wouldn't people just leave my illness alone? I mean, I wasn't going to hurt anybody. In one incident, I was doing an exam, and, because of my ADHD, I had a scribe reader. This means I would answer the questions verbally, but somebody did the writing for me. As always, I tried my best in the test and did what the teacher told me to do, with the teaching assistant as the scribe.

However, to my amazement at break time, many students came up to me saying that I had cheated and that my scribe reader had done the test for me. This made me really sad, as I worked so hard for this test. I was confused because I didn't know what was wrong with me. All I knew was that I struggled to focus and found it hard to learn and remember what the teacher was telling me. Yes, I know it's called ADHD, but I am normal, like everybody else, right? Yes I take medication and apparently it helps me, but I'm still me. Why do people treat me differently?

So, back to the story. Sorry I got distracted again…I told you I do this!

In the playground at break time, one girl said, "Ha, you can't even do the test on your own DUMBO." And then her friend hit me with the dagger in the heart: "You are DISABLED, you should get a disability card…hahaha." They all laughed at me. This was not nice. It hurt, it really hurt. I had done nothing wrong, and yet I was being punished for just trying my best. Is this what the future held for me?

All of this simply made me very sad, and whenever I felt this way at school I would go and sit at the bottom of the stairs with the front door open and hope to catch hypothermia. Yes, I know what you are thinking, this is a silly thing to do, but you don't know how I felt. The constant pain I suffered from people treating me like I had an illness or something. I just wanted out of this school, it was full of people who gave me a hard time because of my so-called disability, disorder or whatever you want to call it. I simply despised this feeling and I would do anything to get rid of it, ANYTHING!

> If only my teachers had asked me how I was. If only somebody could hear my pain and *listen* to me.

I just couldn't get my head around it all. What was I doing wrong? Was I giving them a reason to treat me like this? One thing I did know was that it could not continue as it was. Either they would change or something would have to change within me.

A few years later, when I learned about depression, I was thinking that, yes, this was exactly what I had. How could I have learned anything in this mental state? Why were people not helping me more? How could people be so horrible? When I reflect back it still upsets me. If only my teachers had asked me how I was. If only somebody could hear my pain and *listen* to me.

Points to consider:

- Did you notice an absence of communication in this story?

- Daria mentioned that other people are not understanding or supportive with regards to her disorder. Why do you think she feels this way?

- Daria didn't share her pain with others. Could you guess why this may be the case?

- Imagine if you were Daria; how would you be feeling day after day dealing with this at school?

- Is there anything in Daria's control to improve her relationship with Miss Baker?

- What has to change for Daria to be happier in school?

What does the CMB Wellbeing Warrior say?

Daria made some powerful statements throughout her story. For example: "I felt like this was an attack on me, as if the teacher was jealous of my happiness," "I see pity, anger and disappointment," "It's just not fair," and, "I felt so victimised."

When you are reading this, what are you hearing? Who is Daria 'being' in this instance? Words like this are very common during the first coaching session.

As a coach, I personally like to provide space for the client to express such feelings. After this is done, then we can get to work!

With regards to the statements, I would ask Daria to describe exactly the 'character' she is channelling when feeling and behaving like this, and what outcomes follow. We would then give this character a name, for example, let's call her 'Zoe'.

In short, the idea here is to recognise when Zoe manifests and what triggers her to enter the room. Once we know what Zoe's behaviour is and what feelings are associated with it, we can then do something about it.

Firstly, I can imagine if Daria was to approach me as a client, she would be focusing a lot on her ADHD. Take a look back to the beginning of the story; this is exactly what she did. It is very common for a client to begin a coaching journey wanting to discuss 'their problem', or in this case, a medical condition. This is OK initially, but eventually as coaches, we would redirect the topic and focus on moving away from the problem.

I have had many clients with certain medical conditions, sometimes conditions I know nothing about. I would research them before working with a client, but this is for my own knowledge only. In reality, a coach does not need to be an expert in any field; that's the role of a consultant, or a mentor to some extent.

We want to get the coaching conversation away from the 'condition' and focus more on the potential steps forward. To achieve this, a coach would simply need to ask the correct question, and create a platform using a range of skills to support their client in empowering themselves to design their own path to success.

Daria highlighted at the end of the story that something had to change, so let's start by looking within. I would begin by asking Daria questions regarding what is in her control to change.

We want to guide the conversation to where Daria can start to reflect on her own behaviour, as opposed to that of others. We want her to realise that she cannot control those around her, but by exploring what she can do, we can identify opportunities for change to take place.

Some powerful questions could consist of: "Who do you want to be at school?", "How can you show other people who you really are?" and, "How do you need to present yourself in order to allow your true self to be acknowledged?"

When achieving the above, Daria needs to consider her state. There are many ways your state can be defined, but to put it simply, it is the particular condition that you are in at a specific time.

Through the *CMB Time and Tested State System*, we would identify what state Daria needs to be in, in order to approach school differently. With this, we can examine Daria's physical presence, which includes her stance, tone, energy and general movement when interacting with others. In addition to this, we explore her focus and finally, we consider her language. Essentially we are attempting to create a 'better person' who can conduct herself differently from 'Zoe'. Again, we can give this 'better person' a name and play with their personality across different environments. We can explore what works and what does not.

Daria said that she wants people to listen to her. For this, again we need to look within and see what she can do to make this happen. This can start with her state! Here, we can use Daria's new state to develop how she interacts with others. Once this is mastered, Daria will be in a better position to engage with others and ask for help if and when needed.

Enquiry Questions:

Imagine that you are Daria. You have worked successfully on your state and are now feeling much more confident when interacting with others. What would you like to do with your newfound state? What options are out there, and what would a good outcome be?

CMB Task:

What do you notice about your own state? Can you describe how you think you come across to other people?

Ask! Pick a friend and ask them to describe 'YOU'. Get them to describe your physiology, your energy, and generally how you appear to them. Be prepared, this may be uncomfortable, as you may hear things you don't want to! Examine their responses and see if anything within you needs to change.

15

Ibrahim: My Invisible Presence

I'm not sure what is wrong with me. I don't know why people don't want to be my friend, but that's the way it is. Hi. My name is Ibrahim. I'm 15 years old, but my parents treat me like I'm 5! Well, at least my mum does. As for my dad, when he is around we have a laugh, but that's not very often as he is always away working. Unfortunately, I only see him every few weeks.

Honestly, I'm a nice person, I really am. Nobody seems to see this though. It makes me sad and it makes me doubt myself. The way I am treated at home certainly makes me question my own capabilities. I don't get to have a say in anything, I'm never asked what I think. I'm controlled fully by my mum, fully!

Let me give you an example. Would you believe that my mum still sets up play-dates with people from my class? Yes, I actually said that; how embarrassing! Remember my age? These are people who don't even speak to me at school, and who I know don't want to be friends with me. It's forced and we all know it is. I tell my mother not to do it, but she still does. It's really not helpful, it's actually really shameful. If only she would *listen* to me.

Imagine this: me going round to some guy's house, a guy who doesn't speak to me at school. He plays the PlayStation, and I'm just left sitting there on the bed, silently twiddling my thumbs. I'm not wanted, I get it. I'm better than this. I'm better in my own company than stuck here. At least I respect myself!

As my mother drops me off, she <u>TELLS</u> me, "Go on, make an effort and be friends with him, make him like you."

If only she would *listen* to me.

Eh...what? Did I hear that correctly? What are you trying to pull mum? I am a human being! I have feelings! I know he doesn't like me, so please don't shove it in my face. I actually don't like him either. Just get over it mum, after all, I have. I accept things for the way they are. Please can you just do the same?

This is what I want to say!

I have tried, I really have, but not once has she ever asked me what I want. Not once has she ever asked if I'm OK, or how I feel about this. She has never involved me in the decision-making process, never.

Mum, how about this for a suggestion? How about asking me what I like doing? No, you are always off working. You and dad, never around. I literally don't know if you know who I am. Maybe I'm like this because of you. Maybe the reason I'm a loner at school is because I'm a loner at home. Who do I have to communicate with apart from Rover?

Rover is my dog and best friend. I love him, but how pathetic is it of me to have one friend, an animal! But, you know what, he is always there for me and never lets me down. Rover and I do everything together. He gets me. We play, we laugh, we hug and we sit together for hours, just enjoying each other's company.

I do believe that my social awkwardness is all down to this. From a human perspective, I have nobody to talk to at home, and this leads to having nobody to talk to at school. I am shy because of it. I don't get to communicate with anyone, I don't get to practise these skills. I wish I could be as relaxed with people as I am with Rover.

In class, I'm quiet. I am always shy about participating in classroom activities or engaging in conversations. When the teachers ask me a question I go bright red, my heart pounds and I mix up my words. Even when I know the answer, I never say it. I just doubt myself. Many times I say to myself, *Go for it Ibrahim, do it.* I sit and think about it. My heart starts racing and then 'BOOM', someone else answers it. *Another opportunity gone!*

This is very frustrating when I have the right answer, but it's good when my answer is wrong! When I am right, I beat myself up for not putting my hand up. However, when I am wrong I'm relieved. Saved. *Thank God you didn't say it, you fool!*

And then, the usual personal guilt and judgement enters my head. I feel bad for not engaging, again and again. Over and over, I judge myself and call myself names: *You idiot Ibrahim. Why didn't you just answer it?* Then, another voice will say, *Forget about it, you're just not good enough, you don't have the skills.* And that's me. There you have it, as clear as day. Say hello to the three 'people' in my life: a voice judging me, a voice protecting me, and Rover!

I do try though, I do. One time, Johnny, one of the boys in my class, was having a birthday party. Of course, mum wanted me to go, and obviously I didn't want to. But I did go. I told myself to step out of my comfort zone, it was time to do something about my friendship situation. Sure, what was the worst that could happen, right? Mmmmm…let's see!

The day before the party, I had to buy Johnny a gift. Spending money on Johnny was actually killing me. We were at the shop and my mum was picking out things to buy. I'm there thinking, wow, I would love that gift. If only you would buy that for me mum! I knew what she was doing: she was trying to impress him and win him over by buying the best gift. I might be a loner, but I'm not stupid!

Anyway, we get there and everything is great. He welcomes me with a smile and thanks me for the gift. This alone was different to his usual behaviour towards me, it was a major change from the 'welcome' I always get at school. *OK,* I think to myself, *maybe today is the beginning of a new relationship!*

My mum eventually leaves and all the boys and some girls are hanging out in the garden. I stand at the kitchen table and begin to eat food. Some nice sandwiches and lemonade to be precise. In my awkward stance, I just keep eating and drinking, as I don't know what else to do. Don't get me wrong, the food is great, but I am just waiting for somebody to invite me outside to hang out with Johnny and the other boys.

As time goes on I'm feeling lost, ignored and alone in the same place. "Get me out of here," I say to myself under my breath. I'm actually non-existent to everybody, I'm invisible.

What to do? I really don't know. OK, let's do it, I'm going outside to talk to the boys. But as I approach, some of the boys start looking at me. Then a few sniggers, before one of the boys asks the dreaded question:

"Hey loner, who invited you here?"

Everybody starts to laugh. I nervously say, "Hey everyone," but, as I'm in mid-sentence, literally everybody turns their back on me and just carries on doing what they were doing! Again, left standing there on my own, alone as always. 'Ibrahim the loner!'

Another group in the corner calls me over. "Ibrahim," they say, "come here to us."

Great, I'm saved, I get a sense of relief, somebody actually wants to talk to me. As I get closer they are all lining up, strangely preparing for something. Then one boy called Paulie says, "Take my phone and take a picture of us lads, will you?" I'm gobsmacked; it's literally an order, a dictation! Not only am I ignored, but I'm now also being used as a photographer!

I don't have the energy to argue. I take the picture and walk back inside. I go upstairs to the bathroom. I sit on the toilet with my head in my hands and cry. I don't mean to cry but I just can't help it. I look at my watch and I'm longing for the time to go by. Frustratingly, there are still two hours to go before mum comes to pick me up.

I'm feeling angry and impatient, so I've decided I can't wait. I need to take control, so I go. I leave the party and I just walk, walk and continue to walk. I don't care what my mother will say. Maybe she will see that I just don't fit in and accept it, as I have done.

I'm not in a good place. I'm emotionally a mess. I'm just sick of this life. As cars drive by, I get strange images of me jumping out in front of them. I create a whole image in my head. I can see myself on the road, the car and the ambulance, I see it all, as clear as day. I think to myself:

Will this make people take notice of me? Paulie? Johnny? Mum? Yes, maybe this is the only way to get attention from her. Maybe the people at the party will feel guilty for not involving me. This would be a great way to punish them all, right?

Obviously, I wouldn't do it, I couldn't. It would kill my parents, well, at least I think it would anyway…

After walking for some time, my phone rings. It's my mum. "Here we go," I say, as I know what to expect from her. She asks for my location and I tell her. "OK, I'll be there in 20 minutes," she says in a surprisingly friendlier tone than usual.

A little while later, I see my mother's car approaching. I'm nervous. Nervous and embarrassed about the situation. I have let her down, again. She pulls up beside me, then reaches across the passenger seat to open the door. Out jumps Rover. Oh, I am happy to see him. He leaps up on me and literally holds me, just like a hug. This feels good. How does he know I needed this so much? I look at mum, she appears different to normal. Less straight-faced and more of a sincere presence about her. I get into the car and for the first time EVER, something bizarre happens. My mum looks at me and asks softly:

"Are you OK Ibrahim?"

I look at her with relief, massive relief. She finally sees me. Maybe now she is ready to listen to me.

Points to consider:

- Reflecting on what you have learned from this book, what skills or activities do you think would benefit Ibrahim here?

- Regarding Rover, Ibrahim's 'best friend', can you relate to how he feels about him? What is special, and what is concerning about this relationship?

- Ibrahim mentioned jumping in front of a car. Considering the responses to previous stories that involved suicidal thoughts, how should we advise Ibrahim here?

- Ibrahim's Dad appears to be absent in the story; what effect might this have on Ibrahim?

- Did you feel the power of a hug from Rover? Who in your life needs a hug today?

- At the end of the story, Ibrahim's mum asks him if he's OK. He feels relieved at being asked; how might he have responded?

What does the CMB Wellbeing Warrior say?

Ibrahim openly demonstrates a range of different emotions in this story. What do you think they are? There is also a large amount of agony with regards to his loneliness, which is made evident when he describes his dog Rover as his 'best friend'.

However, there is a visible strength within Ibrahim. Statements such as: "I respect myself," "I need to get out of my comfort zone," "I accept things for the way they are," and, "I need to take control," indicate that we have some great resources to work with here.

As a coach in this instance, it would be valuable to focus the energy of the conversation on such positives, in order to create an environment where Ibrahim feels good about himself. This alone will build trust and team cohesion, key ingredients in a successful coaching relationship.

There is a clear sense of mum versus Ibrahim in this story. However, if we take a step back and try to see it from his mother's perspective, what do you think her agenda is?

Is she really the enemy, or is it love and kindness that is the driving force behind everything she does?

During a coaching session, this is something we could explore further, where we attempt to see it all through the lens of mum. We briefly touched on this earlier with Livia in Chapter 7.

This is conducted through the *CMB Practical Exchange Principle*. Here, we step into the shoes of mum and examine her intentions. This will bring a new appreciation to the situation and bridge the 'me versus her' attitude, and therefore form an alliance between them both. We would look at what Ibrahim can do in order to start constructing this bridge, as he is the client. The reality is that life would be easier for Ibrahim if they were on the same wavelength, so let's do whatever it takes to make this happen.

It is in our personal interest to have those close to us on board with what we want to do. This realisation is important here, as it allows Ibrahim to have a teammate on board where he can possibly share his intentions, collaborate on plans and receive feedback or guidance if desired.

A trusted companion always comes in handy, whether it's a family member, a classmate, a teacher, a co-worker or a friend. Having someone to help tackle your challenges can have a positive influence on your actions. It can bring a sense of security to whatever it is you are trying to achieve.

I personally use this approach with the most important decisions I make. When doing this, selecting the right people is key, and you will eventually find out who the right people are based on past conversations and the results which followed! Fundamentally, the end decision or action still lies with you, but listening to other opinions can add great value to the way you feel before proceeding.

Another area of focus here could be Ibrahim's communication with others. Through advanced exploration and with the development of his communications skills, Ibrahim would be able to effectively communicate his feelings to another person. This was evidently missing from his story, and I could sense a clear frustration where this is concerned. By being able to communicate better, he would naturally function better.

With this newfound change of perspective from Ibrahim, and a new approach with regards to communication, Ibrahim would enable his feelings to be heard, felt and acknowledged.

Simple things like this have a major impact on the relationships teenagers have with their parents. An understanding is created, which works both ways! It's never easy for both parties, and it takes teamwork to make the relationship a successful one. Together is stronger!

Similar communication skills can be used with regards to Ibrahim's engagement with people at school. In this instance, we could break down the situations he finds himself in and build a hypothetical response for each identified problem, leading to a new 'learned behaviour' for future challenges. For example, we would work on how Ibrahim could conduct himself around others and how to present himself when speaking in front of the class. Here, Ibrahim would learn how to 'be', when in situations he finds challenging, and establish how to approach such challenges in order to get more desirable results. During this 'exploration mode', he would learn to perceive each challenge with a less rational, less blameless manner, therefore demonstrating a more empathetic attitude toward himself.

An unusual ingredient here is to have a sense of humour over his misfortunes. It is understandable to react to failure with negative emotion, as Ibrahim did in his story. However, sometimes, by not taking ourselves too seriously, we can get over disappointments much faster and, therefore, begin to forward-think and re-plan. This alone is very powerful.

Enquiry Question:

Imagine that Ibrahim has now developed his skills, where he can explore other perspectives and be more aware of how to 'be' when engaging with others. What do you think is the first thing he would want to target? Think about what is important to him!

CMB Task:

Reflect back to a time when somebody else attempted to control your actions. Write down what you think their intentions were. Now, put yourself in their shoes and explore the perspective through their eyes. Think about other possible motives of why they are guiding you towards a certain direction. Write these down also, then step back and review. What happens when you shift your mode of thinking to one that is less defensive?

16

Holly: The Harsh Reality Of Distance Learning

*L*et's face it, 2021 has been a difficult year. Not just for me, but for many people throughout the world. My dad lost his job, and mum was working from home every day. My brother Tom and I were distance learning. It was a complete nightmare. Let's just say the concoction of it all was disastrous in the end. From a perfect family to a disjointed family…to put it mildly!

It is such a relief to finally express how this all has affected me. I couldn't speak to my family, they were too caught up in it all, they wouldn't *listen* anyway!

Dad: My dad is a proud man, a good person and a very loving father and husband. However, being at home unearthed a completely distinctive side to him, he was a different dad to what we are used to. Before I tell you all about his flaws of late, let me build you a picture of his normal self; who he was, my dad, my 'super dad'.

Dad is a successful person. He is good at his job and very talented in everything he does. We were always financially free and he would do anything for us. We would go on family holidays at least twice a year and we always had what we needed. Good food, clothes, health, you name it, if we needed it, dad would sort it. I'm not saying we were super-rich, but we were comfortable. Dad worked hard, for hours on end for his boss. He loved it though, and was very committed to his team at work.

> I couldn't speak to my family, they were too caught up in it all, they wouldn't *listen* anyway!

When we go out for dinner or events, dad is always Mr. Popular. People seem to be attracted to him, he has great energy and offers so much life to whatever social company he is in. When he comes home from work, the house comes alive and we all have a ball together. He gives us everything, from love and care, to safety and adventure.

Dad is athletic, 'fresh' for his age. My friends always comment on how he looks: "Oh Holly, I saw your dad today…looooooooking goooooooood." I get this a lot, it is very much uncomfortable, awkward in fact! But, in fairness to him, he looks after himself well. I would say he is a modern man, contemporary and stylish. He exercises every day, mainly running and swimming and is very much into mental wellbeing. He is a great believer in talking openly and challenging problems collectively together. Life is never lonely when dad is present, and no challenge is ever too big. Well, that's what I thought!

Covid comes along and dad's company is hit hard. He is furloughed without any financial support. To make it worse we go into a major lockdown. Week after week goes by, and still no developments. Watching the news daily is soul-destroying as the statistics just keep getting worse globally. Dad is now at home all day. This is not good for him, he needs to be active and engaging with others. I can sense that something is changing in him, and not in a good way.

At the start of lockdown, dad was very positive and said things like, "We need to use this as a gift, it's a rest from the real world." He was home training every day, sometimes even twice, cooking healthy food and spending his time reading self-help books, or watching educational documentaries on TV. It was as if the difficulties associated with lockdown were having a positive effect on him, it really was.

However, after time (around the two month mark) his behaviour begins to change. He is staying up late and getting out of bed really late. He doesn't shave, he looks a mess in fact. He is negative, tense and has an anxious feeling about him, all day, every day. He is not himself, he is lost. I look at him with complete sympathy. Where has my dad gone? Seeing his decline is heartbreaking.

Mum: Mum is a wonderful mum, honestly she is. Working long hours and playing long hours. She loves to exercise, so as soon as she is home, she is straight out again, either to the gym or just for a run. I join her sometimes. She is my role model and when I grow up, I want to be just like her. Yes, I know what you are thinking, the usual cliché, but if I had her personality, drive and energy, I would be completely fulfilled in life. She looks after herself well and is not afraid to spend money on life's luxuries!

Like dad, work changed for her. Firstly, it was working from home. Initially we were selfishly delighted with this, as we had our mum at home all day, but frustratingly it didn't work out this way. We literally never saw her. Bizarrely, even though she didn't have to go into the office, it seemed that she had never been so busy. It was like she was always on call. Over breakfast, lunch and dinner, mum was on the phone or laptop.

Mum being busy started to really get to us all, dad especially. "Can you not for one minute just spend time with us?" he would ask her. Deep down I think there was some sort of jealousy present, or maybe embarrassment, yes, embarrassment sounds more accurate. I know dad just wanted to be the breadwinner, but he wasn't. This was hurting him badly. Mum was in charge now!

Mum would get up early, exercise, wash and get ready for work. She would do her hair and makeup, put on a lovely shirt and, peculiarly, wear tracksuit bottoms. Yes, you heard me right, trust me she did. During her online meetings, she looked great, just like a news presenter, but off screen a bit idiotic to be perfectly honest! It was funny though, she would even put on perfume for goodness sake. "C'mon mum," I would say, "nobody can smell you through the computer screen." Mum is quite the performer. Great energy, great talent, great looking and simply a wonderful mum. Like dad, she would do anything for us.

Mum has a good job also. Pre-Covid, I wouldn't say she was married to her job, but it did take up a lot of her time. She is a modern woman. She is educated and had a successful career before Tom and I came along. Tom is my brother. Mum took time out of work to be a full-time mum, until we were old enough to go to school, when she began to work again. A perfect situation really. We now have a nanny who helps out with the household chores, and supports school preparation etc. We are privileged, I admit that, and I am amazingly grateful for everything we have.

But Covid had a negative effect on my mum also. It started with the pressures from work. Colleague after colleague would video call her non-stop, all the time, looking for support. They were having their own challenges due to Covid, so mum was a great help to them. She is a very supportive and understanding person. She really wants to help them and gives them all the time they need. However, soon we started to wonder what her priority was, her family or her colleagues. It felt like they were always present in our home, only an on-screen version of people we do not know.

Day after day this was happening. It was like she was some sort of counsellor or something. In amongst all this, she actually had to get her own work done. She was now working longer hours than she did when she was working from the office, it was getting crazy. She was up until all hours of the night, and then the next day was a repeat. Daily, the same thing was happening. Our weekends were also being destroyed, it was as if 24 hours on weekdays just wasn't enough. She was a woman in demand. People were taking away my mother, my father's wife, and we were losing her to strangers. It just wasn't fair. "Why always them and never us?" I would ask. Originally we thought working from home was going to be a good thing for the family, but things are changing now, changing for the worse.

Distance learning: "YES, YES, YES, YES, no more going into school!"

My friends and I were all shouting and screaming when the news broke out back in spring 2020. This was so exciting. We couldn't believe it was happening. There was talk of it a week earlier, but we didn't actually think it would happen. But it did. School is now in my bedroom. Wow, this should be fun, so futuristic. Sadly, after some time, the thrill of distance learning wasn't so thrilling after all!

The first few weeks were good. It was all about getting used to the new software, the new ways of doing things. My teachers were great. They went to considerable lengths to make it work for us. They had backup after backup of ways for us to learn. Everything was catered for. Text instructions, video demonstrations and live lessons. We even had an option to do mindfulness at lunchtimes. It was amazing actually.

PE in my bedroom? The thought of it at first was really weird, but the teacher was so good, so energetic and so creative. In truth, my school did a great job. We were so lucky, thank you to everybody involved.

However, after some time it started to get a bit repetitive. This was understandable. What else could they do? I was sick to the teeth of being on screen. Tired eyes, headaches, not sleeping well. It all got to me. I really think the screen time affected my mental and physical wellbeing. When my friends would want to video call after school, I just wasn't interested. I'd had enough screen time. I didn't want to watch TV, read, or even use social media on my phone.

The combination of living, schooling and working at home all together was the worst part of it all. Picture this: there we all were, my mum in one bedroom working, myself and Tom at the dining table or in our bedrooms doing our school lessons, and dad on the sofa. For our live lessons, we had to leave the room to go somewhere quiet, but this attracted its own problem: the dreaded loss of internet connection!

"Muuuuuuum, I've lost connection." "Tooooommmmm, get offline, I'm on a call here." This happened hour after hour. The one-to-one meetings with my teachers created their own problems:

"Hello, hello, hello, can you hear me…hello, Holly, are you there?"

"Yes sir, I am here, turn your screen on!"

I would have to say this to him numerous times! Finally, we get to see each other and…FREEZE. There goes the connection again. Nightmare!

This was our normal day, a stressful and challenging one, one day after the next, one week after the next, and one month after the next. I longed to go back to school, back to how it used to be. I never thought I'd say that!

These were tough times for me, for us all. I know I sound selfish, because when I see the news, there are people and whole countries that are in worse situations than us. But still, it's my life, I'm entitled to express how I feel.

Dad seemed depressed, mum was working all day and Tom and I were trying to keep up with school work. It was impossible really. Dad tried to help us, but he didn't know what to do. It was as if he lost his soul, his drive, his motivation and his inner self. Empty, he was simply empty.

Regrettably, we had to let our nanny go for financial reasons. This was hard, as it impacted her family in the Philippines also. The day she left was so sad. We all cried, it was heart-breaking seeing her standing on the other side of the road waiting for a bus to come, holding her one suitcase with all her belongings in it. So many years of service, and gone, just like that. How could we do that to her? This dreaded Covid was killing us, like a curse, killing us slowly inside and outside.

Mum was getting sick of dad's behaviour. He would complain about everything: "There is no milk," "The place is a mess," and the daily reliable, "Where is the bloody remote control?" Without fail, the remote control would get lost!

It was takeaway food most nights. Mum was too busy and dad wasn't interested in cooking anymore. Deliveroo again, here we go. It seemed to be the only time we all communicated actually. Every evening around 5pm, "What will we have for dinner?" That's it though, no more talk after that. The days of collectively sitting over the dinner table and talking were gone. Mum in the bedroom eating on the go and dad on the sofa watching some kind of South American crime drama on Netflix.

There was always something to argue about. Mum would get the blame for most things, but it was never her fault. She would then hit back at dad with, "Why don't you get up and do something you lazy b*****d!"

It was not like her to shout at Dad or demonstrate aggressive and rude behaviour. This concerned me. They began to argue a lot. Day after day there was always something between them, an atmosphere, a negative vibe or something. They stopped communicating and ultimately ignored each other. The house was becoming an uncomfortable place to be in. Tom wouldn't say much, I found him in his bedroom crying a few times but he never said why. Deep down I could tell, I knew exactly what he was thinking and feeling. Our family was falling apart. Bit by bit, what we used to have was being taken away from us. Damn you Covid!

This is home life now. Not so perfect anymore. My dad is still out of work and mum is still very busy. We are lucky that we have one income to pay for our schooling and everything else, but we are just getting by. In fact, our school payments were late and I couldn't actually access the software, as I was taken off the register. This was embarrassing, my school absence was due to us not paying the fees. Try telling that to those who ask! No more holidays, no more fancy restaurants and no more buying clothes. But what good is money if we have no family bond, no love, and, as it currently feels, no hope? I don't know what the future holds for us. I'm wishing to wake up one day and find out that this is all a nightmare. Feel free to pinch me.

Points to consider:

- Can you relate to Holly's story here, or elements of it?

- Holly's dad has had a complete fall from grace. Can you imagine what he is feeling? What would you like to say to him? What would help him?

- Regarding Holly's mother, how do you think she is currently feeling?

- Can you envisage being part of a household that bears so much negativity?

- From the outside looking in, what do you think is the way forward for Holly and her family?

- As for Holly, it sounds like the story is very much about her family, but what about her feelings and experiences throughout this time? How could this all affect her?

What does the CMB Wellbeing Warrior say?

I think it's fair to say that Holly's Covid-19 experience is a familiar story, one shared by many people globally. As a coach, it would be advisable, however, not to make Holly feel that her pain is commonplace, and that many others are experiencing the same distress. Can you guess why this is the case?

Have you ever told somebody a personal issue and they responded with, "Yeah, it's the same for me," or "But look at other people, they have it much worse than you!"? Statements like these are not always helpful, and can cause feelings of mental deflation, as the person may feel that their claims are not being taken seriously. What is key here is to demonstrate empathy, and to be present for Holly, as this conversation is about her and her alone. Of course, perspective can be used here, but first we must engage and listen to people when they are trying to openly communicate their personal grievances to us.

Hypothetically speaking, if Holly came to a coaching session with this story, she would have many topics to discuss. She has expressed concern about her dad and his downfall, her mum and her long hours of working from home, her brother and his silence, the guilt of letting her nanny go, the poor relationship between mum and dad, and significantly, herself and her own mental and physical wellbeing. In addition to this, there seems to be a frustration with regards to Covid. There is a wave of anger beginning to appear. Did you notice this?

With so many potential topics, it can be difficult for a client to pinpoint the one that needs immediate attention. In this instance, and through the *CMB Grow Rich Appreciation Activator*, Holly can create an awareness about the different aspects of her life that she may want to focus on. For this, I would request that Holly completes an activity that involves a 'Wheel of Life'. Here, Holly can list the identified topics and give them a rating out of ten on how she currently feels about each one. For example, if she is really happy about something, she would give it a high score, whereas if she is unhappy or less fulfilled, it would be a low score. This simple yet extremely effective tool will provide Holly with an overview and clear picture of what areas in her life need prioritising.

The wonderful thing about this activity is that it provides clients with a visual and demonstrates certain imbalances that need particular attention. It's a great tool to begin a coaching journey with. Furthermore, it can be used uniquely to suit the specific needs of the client. For example, with many clients, I have adapted the

'Wheel of Life' to a 'Wheel of School' for students having difficulty in certain aspects of school life, a 'Wheel of Work' for people experiencing challenges at work, and a 'Wheel of Emotions' for those having emotional difficulty. The results from this activity lay down the foundations for the next coaching session.

Enquiry Question:

If you were Holly and your parents were constantly arguing, what is in your power to support the situation?

CMB Task:

Create your own 'Wheel of Life'. Make a list of general areas in your life. Select at least eight. For example, school, recreation, relationships, health etc. and rate them out of 10. Examine the end product and see what areas you are not feeling fulfilled in.

Now, attempt to answer the following questions:

- What is your topic?

- What are you currently feeling about _____?

- What do you really want from _____?

- What is important to you about _____?

- How can you improve the situation for _____?

- What is stopping you from doing this?

- What options are available to you?

- What are you willing to do next?

- How will you hold yourself accountable?

- How will you measure its success?

17

Charlie: Who Chooses My Future, Me Or My Parents?

Throughout high school, I had to juggle many expectations from my parents, like most people I suppose. Towards the end of my school years, this pressure began to get unbearable, I just couldn't keep up with it all.

My name is Charlie. I'm a 17-year-old boy preparing for my life ahead. Ah, that sounds so weird saying that, 'MY LIFE'. It certainly doesn't feel like it's my life, if I am being totally honest. Let me tell you why.

My parents never gave me a break. They were always on my case. Grades, grades and grades, that's all I ever got at home. Look, I'm blessed, I know I am. I go to a private school in an amazing city. My parents work hard to pay for it and believe me, it doesn't come cheap! I have amazing facilities and the best learning environment a student could ask for. I appreciate what my parents do for me, trust me, I really do. They invest a lot in me, providing it's educational, or that some sort of learning is taking place.

I know what you are thinking. You're thinking I'm fortuitous and that I have nothing to complain about. But please, believe me, I'm not complaining, I'm not. I just want my side of things to be heard. Is this too much to ask for? I'm grateful for everything I have. I'm also grateful to have an opportunity to express myself right here, right now. You will see in my story why this was so important for me in order to move forward in my life. Yes, MY LIFE!

So back to my parents. They work hard. They are educated and ambitious. They are both medical doctors. Can you guess what profession they want me to be in? Yep…they want me to be a doctor, just like them and just like my grandparents. But you know what? I have absolutely no interest in becoming a doctor. It's as simple as that. I love sports. I want to work in the sports industry. But no, I don't have a choice. I have to apply for medical school.

I have experienced great success in school sports. I also received top marks for my GCSEs in PE, but was forced to drop it by my parents, in order to study something more 'academic' that will serve my future better! C'mon, what is this all about? Aren't parents supposed to support their children? Want the best for them? Want to see them happy? Clearly not in my case.

It's all very pressuring, not just for me, but for my teachers also. Picture this: it's parents evening and both my parents attend. To their credit not all parents do, so I feel supported. My teachers are amazing, lovely people who genuinely care about me. Both my parents always come into the meeting with an attitude however, I can feel the tension. It's as if they are talking down to the teachers. Like, what's this about? My teachers are professionally qualified, they work extremely hard and go to great lengths to help me, and yet my parents come out with some ridiculous questions: "Why this grade?", "Why no assessment recently?" and, "Why is Charlie's friend getting higher grades?"

I sit there with embarrassment, I really do. I just want the floor to eat me up. My teachers can tell what I'm thinking, we are on the same page. As for my parents, they are on another planet!

Then there are all my personal tutors. I literally have a tutor for every subject. Again, I appreciate this extra support, but as a substitute for what? My childhood? OK, I'm not a child, but you know what I mean. All my friends hit the park or the shops after school. But for me, it's into the books again. I just never get a break. I go to a homework club on the weekends and my parents enrol me in summer school. What happened to being an all-round student? I'm told this is what successful people are, all-rounders!

How can I develop other skills if all I am doing is studying? I literally never get any opportunities to develop other aspects of myself and who I need to be in order to take on the real world outside of school. Organisation skills, teamwork skills, communication skills, and the rest. No, no room for that in this hectic schedule, it's books, books and more depressing books.

The stress and anxiety I experience in the build-up to my exams is just enormous, and it gets worse when I'm awaiting the results. There are times when I cannot breathe. I sit in my bedroom and hope, simply hope to get what I deserve. I would actually say that the pressure and resulting stress levels have a negative impact on my performance. I mean, how can I concentrate under such pressurised circumstances? I wish my parents knew the strain they were putting me under. If only they would ask how I was feeling, if only they would *listen*!

I work extremely hard, so I feel I do deserve my desired outcomes, but it doesn't always work out like this. There are times when I don't get the results my parents and I are hoping for. This is never good. When this happens my house turns into a police interrogation room. "Why, why and why?" I reckon this is the most used word in their vocabulary.

It's not always my fault though. Maybe I am just not good enough to get the results THEY want me to get. Also, let us not forget that I am doing the subjects that THEY selected for me. Can you imagine how different it would have been if I chose the subjects that I wanted? Wow, I wonder what having a voice feels like. I would be studying the subjects that I enjoy, this would add more interest into what I am learning, and I have no doubt my results would be better. Overall, I would be a happier student. Does my happiness and fulfilment not matter to my parents? Surely these are great ingredients for success?

> If only they would ask how I was feeling, if only they would *listen*!

Anyway, the exams arrived, and unfortunately I did not get the results WE wanted. I was finding the subjects too hard and I simply wasn't my usual upbeat self. I'm not one for blaming, but I strongly attribute this to not studying what I wanted to do. I lacked personal drive and motivation, as my future was being decided for me by my parents. I had no say in it. I was no longer looking forward to it. I would be working in an industry that I hated just to meet the expectations of others. Something had to change, I couldn't continue like this. I really wanted to tell them how I was feeling, but I felt pangs of tremendous guilt that I would let them down.

I arranged a meeting with a teacher I trust. I explained everything to him and expressed my true feelings. He understood my perspective. He is a smart guy and he felt confident that if we had a meeting, all of us together, we could open up some other options for me.

The next day we all sat down. Again, my parents were not in the most 'welcoming' kind of mood, as they were not in control for once. Anyhow, my teacher got his point across on my behalf in a friendly way and opened the floor for me to speak. Very tellingly,

I was nervous. For the first time, in my parents' presence, I had a platform to express how I felt.

To my amazement, they actually listened to me, they really did! I was so relieved. I could feel my whole body relax as they listened. The anxious pain in my chest was leaving me for the first time in years. An enormous weight was lifted as soon as I expressed what I wanted to. This was simply amazing! Even if nothing changed, I was still satisfied just to have a voice, to give my perspective and to share my feelings on the matter.

Thankfully, things did change. That meeting was the start of me taking control of my life. The energy I felt and the excitement I had to take action was immense. After further conversations, I decided not to go down the medical career path and redirected my plans to where I wanted them to go.

My school was really supportive and, with some adjustments and major flexibility by my teachers, I am now studying the subjects that I want to study. The ones I enjoy, the ones I am passionate about. And, guess what? My grades are improving and I am actually enjoying school! Notably, I'm now looking forward to my future. I explored a career path that suited my personal ambitions first and foremost. A career that would allow me to pursue my passions, while still ticking the practical boxes of things I enjoy doing.

I now plan to study Sports Science at university. I cannot tell you how excited I am to be able to say this. I have a new incentive to do well, a new desire to learn and a great commitment to my lessons. I am so eager to be prepared for the next chapter in my life; it's in my control now, and I <u>will</u> make it work.

It is amazing how things have turned around in the last few months. To my relief, the stress and anxiety have left me and I'm living a much happier life, a more fulfilled and balanced life.

Ultimately, my parents only ever wanted me to be successful, and have been entirely supportive of my new choice and career path ever since that meeting with my teacher. I am very grateful to have had the opportunity to express my own desires and take control of my own life. My parents have listened to me. If only I'd spoken to them sooner.

Points to consider:

- What was stopping Charlie from talking to his parents earlier? What do you think their agenda was?

- What skills do you now know to find this out?

- Did you notice what happened to Charlie physically when he expressed what he did to his parents? How might you have reacted?

- What role did Charlie's teacher play here? What skills did he use?

- Regarding Charlie's behaviour, what has changed and how will this impact his future?

- What is now possible for Charlie from the current situation?

What does the CMB Wellbeing Warrior say?

This exact story is something I have heard many times throughout my teaching and coaching career. Luckily for Charlie, it worked out for him, but this is not always the case for students who experience constant pressure from parents.

As you read through Charlie's story, you wouldn't be alone by wanting to say, "Why don't you just tell your parents how you feel?" This sounds like the most sensible thing to do, right? However, we don't know the difficulty Charlie has had with this. As a coach, it is not wise to say it as WE see it. If we do, it turns into OUR agenda, and not that of the client's.

Looking back at the story, there is an agenda that is held by Charlie's parents. However, as Charlie's coach, I would certainly not be putting the blame on them, after all, they would want what's best for him. Wouldn't they…?

Similar to Livia and Ibrahim's stories, I would firstly work on Charlie gaining an appreciation for his parents' perspective and to consider how they feel about the matter. Clearly, they are passionate about the medical profession and this is where we could start.

Once Charlie can give some recognition to his parents' mindset on this particular situation, he can then approach them with a better understanding of how they feel. Charlie can demonstrate empathy and sincerity, as opposed to coming across aggressively, defensively and selfishly in their eyes. This new approach should provide the basis for a more open and fair conversation and decrease the chance of conflict. Remember the 'bridge' example? The stronger your bridge with others, the easier your life will be!

Another angle that could be utilised here is bringing them all together through the use of a mediator, similar to what Charlie's teacher did, only this time using a more 'coaching' manner. This is where an independent person, 'the mediator', is present, to help them discuss and resolve their differences. In order for this to be successful, the mediator needs to be approved by all parties involved, where they will enter the conversation from a neutral stance and form no bias towards any members. In this case, the mediator would be the coach.

With the communication 'bridge' between Charlie and his parents under construction, the mediator idea could be something that Charlie initiates through his improved manner of communicating when speaking to them.

In Charlie's story, his teacher used this method and it worked. It must be noted, however, that this doesn't always demonstrate success and can even sometimes make the situation worse. All parties involved must want to be part of a conversation like this and be open to a shift in their way of thinking on the matter. If this is not the case, another approach would be advisable.

From my experience, providing a platform for everybody to have their say in an organised fashion with the use of a 'facilitator' can work wonders to help repair relationships. The skills of a productive conversation such as this can be learned and performed through the *CMB Group Roadmap Resolution*. Here, the clients would consist of all the people involved in the conflict, or to put it differently, a contrast of opinions! They would all come to a coaching session together and complete the task in each other's presence.

When conducting this, I would start by outlining behaviour expectations devised and agreed upon by each participant before commencing, just like in Chapter 6. Can you recall the name of this?

In this setting, with regards to behaviour, I use the term 'expectations', as opposed to 'rules'. 'Rules' offer less flexibility, whereas 'expectations' provide all participants with autonomy to change something if needed. Once this is done, we would be ready to proceed to talking and listening.

Each person will express how they feel. The person listening will then respond and convey the situation from their viewpoint. Once it is felt that everyone has been given a fair opportunity to express themselves, we move onto the next stage. This involves all parties demonstrating a show of appreciation to each person's perspective on the matter, and cohesively exploring steps to positively move forwards. This model can take some time, and there are various methods to conduct it.

In a separate coaching session, I could work with Charlie's parents alone. In this instance, going by how the story unfolded, I would guess that there would be a specific focus on their controlling element over his future. Here, we would explore their agenda, where I would call upon our imaginary friend again, the *CMB Space Invader*, and involve a controlling character called the 'Reckless Ruler'.

On an occasion like this, instead of me forcing them to let go of their control, we would examine what control means to them. It can be common for people to have difficulty letting go of their own views, as it can be seen as demonstrating encouragement of the opposite opinion, so the coach has to be sensible on how to manage a session such as this.

Examination and deeper understanding of what control means to Charlie's parents would unearth new meanings and create an appreciation and reasoning behind the importance of this stance. We could then explore this stance through the various coaching tools and discover a new appreciation of what a shift in behaviour would achieve, not only for them, but also for Charlie.

Enquiry Questions:

How do you think Charlie's parents are feeling now? Disappointed, happy, or somewhere in between? Do you think the outcome is worth them giving Charlie control of the situation?

CMB Task:

Think of a situation in your own life where you have had a personal agenda and tried to control the other person into doing what 'you' wanted them to do. After seeing the outcome of Charlie's story, do you have a different perspective now? If you were to experience this again, what could you do differently to make the outcome a better one for the other person?

18

Waleed: My Weight Problem And Class Clown Act!

Hello. My name is Waleed. I was a unique child, not very popular at first, but wanted to be different from the rest. I felt that I needed to stand out and be accepted into social groups, so I did things that were, well, on reflection probably a bit stupid. School has had its many ups and downs for me. I will firstly begin with the downs.

I'm fat. Yes, you heard me right, I said fat. Sure, everybody else says it, so I have come to terms with the fact that I'm fat. I'm OK with this. When I look in the mirror I see a fat body, a fat head, fat arms and fat legs, so let's be honest here, I'm fat! In fact, I don't recall myself looking any different. My parents are not the lightest either, so that's where I got it from; it's in my genes. It could be argued that our Arabian diet of greasy foods and lack of exercise as a family had a role to play also!

My parents were always generous when it came to food. Take-aways on most nights and leftovers for lunch. It was always so tasty. In primary school, my friends and I would always compare lunches. They had to eat fruit and stuff and I had lovely seasoned rice and chicken with amazing flavour, washed down with a nice fizzy drink. They were so envious of me. "Waleed, do you want to swap today?"

"Eh, no thanks," I would always say, "I don't think so!"

Everyone wanted my food so much that sometimes I even had to hide away just to eat in peace, really I did. As for exercise, never. Mum would always write me a sick note, as, "PE was just not for you," her words, not mine!

Looking back now, those boys were probably the real lucky ones, with their nice bread, fruit and healthy drinks, and also playing sports inside and outside of school. I'm sure they now have nice athletic bodies and are fit and healthy.

I'm not one to blame others, but I would love to say to my parents:

"What were you thinking, giving me food like that every day and writing me sick notes for PE? What did you expect me to end up like?"

Is it fair to ask such questions? Is my health not their responsibility? I would have thought so!

I have felt frustrated about this ever since I was old enough to have an opinion on it. Yes, I am more educated than them on the matter, but they are neither ancient nor stupid. I have never confronted them about it however, as I'm not sure they would understand.

When I moved up to secondary school, my weight caused many more problems for me. In primary school, it was never really an issue. We had a smaller friendship group, we were who we were and we accepted each other for this. Judgement was not part of our DNA back then, so we all just got on with each other in a carefree environment. In secondary school, things were somewhat different. Fat boy, fatty, chunks, meaty and sumo, yes, I was called them all, and more! The most awkward one was to be called after the Science teacher in school, Mr. Roberts, because he was fat. "Hey Roberts!" I was referred to by some students. It was not pleasant.

Names were, and still are, hard to deal with. I consider this bullying, from an emotional perspective. I told my teachers many times, but nothing came of it, they didn't *listen!* School never really took my complaints too seriously. In fact, I used to wish that these bullies would beat me up! Yes, I really did. I felt that it would give me some physical evidence of the constant torment I experienced day in, day out, where my pain could become visible.

Emotional pain just doesn't seem to attract the same attention, or doesn't seem to be taken as seriously. I was never beaten up, so nothing to show for the bullying, and unfortunately nobody could see the pain inside my body. It was there every day, at home, at school, it was everywhere, it would never leave me. These people who were calling me names, did they know what they were doing to me? I felt sure that one day they would grow up and move on. Well, that's what I hoped anyway.

> I told my teachers many times,
> but nothing came of it, they didn't *listen!*

As time went on, things got worse. Social media came along, and it was this type of bullying that hurt the most. I would randomly get posts sent to me. People thought they were being funny, but they didn't realise what they were doing to me psychologically. I could be sitting at home watching TV when something would happen out of the blue. You know when you are watching something, randomly look at your phone, enter the passcode and then you think to yourself: *Ah, why did I do that? I was perfectly happy watching TV without my phone.* And then there it is. A photo sent to me with my face photoshopped on a fat orangutan, or a sumo wrestler. I could give you many examples, unfortunately.

It got worse than this however. One time at the end of a party, we had a group photo taken of everybody in our class. The photo was posted on social media to everybody in it, including me. But somebody had photoshopped over my face and enlarged my head to make it double the size. I stood out like a sore thumb, me and my bigger, fatter head! No one commented on the actual party, or the photo, all comments were towards me and laughing at me. It was horrendous, really hurtful. Another time when I was in a group photo, somebody photoshopped it by enlarging my belly and putting it in a wheelbarrow that was placed in front of me with a message: 'Sometimes we all need a helping hand to hold ourselves up!!!' This was not nice to experience, not nice at all.

It never ended, there was always something. It was just not fair. When I saw these images, I'd get a horrible pain in my chest and my heart would race. I became afraid to open my phone, but contrary to this, I would get paranoid whenever I was offline, thinking that somebody had posted a photo of me, so I actually found myself checking my phone all the time. It became a habit, a bad habit. It was always there in my head, never going away. I didn't deserve this, I was a good person, I really was.

So what could I do? Well, I asked for help, but nothing happened. So instead I decided to go along with it, to be the funny one, to be who they all wanted me to be, 'the class clown'. If they were going to laugh at me, I might as well have some control, like pretend that I was OK with it…right?

So that's what I did. I rolled with it. I would lift my shirt upon request and shake my fat, just like the guy in the old Goonies movie. I allowed the boys to shoot golf balls off my belly and post it on social media, and yes, I took bets to see how many Big Macs I could eat. I gave them what they wanted, I fed their hunger. Unfortunately for me, I was the starter, main course and dessert!

I know what you are thinking, you're thinking I brought it on myself. You're thinking that I had no self-respect. Well, you know what, you are right to think so: I had <u>zero</u> self-respect. I lost that some time ago when the pain just got so bad. I looked at myself in the mirror one day and the tears were coming down so fast I ran out of tissues. There was no way out for me. I was done. I just had to give up. Give up on fighting back against these bullies, give up on trying to be who I wanted to be, and give in to who society wanted me to be. I accepted defeat; the bullies won. I was fat and they could go ahead and use me for their entertainment. Go on then, feed me to the dogs!

I did mention earlier that there were ups and downs. Refreshingly, it's time for the ups. It wasn't all that bad. I found something I was good at, something that allowed me to show off my 'class clown' performance...DRAMA. Yes, you heard that right.

If you had told me this years before, I would have laughed at you. Actually, when I saw Drama on our school timetable, I distinctly remember myself saying, "THERE'S ABSOLUTELY NO WAY YOU WILL SEE ME ON STAGE, NOT WITH THIS BODY!"

It all started in the school talent show. The boys in my year group dared me to enter it and, as I liked to please others and entertain, I did it. I wanted to make them laugh, make them like me. They dressed me up as a sumo wrestler and we made a home-made version of the trunks. Yes, I stood on stage in front of the whole school wearing only sumo wrestler trunks! We created a dance routine where I had to lift other boys up and kind of be all aggressive and stuff. It was silly really, it wasn't proper drama. But believe it or not, I enjoyed it. There was an element of freeness about it. I felt that I was in a world of my own, even with an assembly full of eyes on me, I felt free, I was at ease, with my body and mind.

The reality was that it was all a big joke. Again, I made many people laugh. I delivered as usual, in fact, I did better than that, the cats got their cream and yes, I was that cream!

But this time was different. OK, I admit, I embarrassed myself, but up on stage, something happened inside me. Something changed where I felt some sort of empowerment. I was different, I had a swagger about me. Afterwards, the drama teacher Mr. Jones came to me and we chatted. I can remember the conversation so vividly, especially his perky posh 'drama darling' voice: "Waleed, you are a joker, but we have something to work with here, there is a talent inside you, we just need to bring it alive."

Wow, somebody had given me a compliment. Literally, this was the first time ever. I had never experienced anything like this before, not even from my parents. This felt nice, I liked it, I wanted more of that please!

This was the start of a special relationship between Mr. Jones and me. He helped with things I was struggling with, such as teaching me how to tie a tie and buying me healthy cereal bars. He even arranged for the PE teacher to create a diet plan for me and immediately I began to see changes. I don't just mean by losing weight, but in my general confidence. My facial skin was even improving, no more spots! He showed me kindness and care. Mr. Jones believed in me.

Maybe this was all I needed throughout my upbringing. Maybe if more of this was present at home, I would have been a stronger person and able to deal with my challenges differently. I will never know. Mr. Jones gave me a lot of his time, as he did for many students. He worked on my communication skills, he taught me how to act, how to present myself in front of an audience and how to demonstrate good manners.

Fast forward a few months and I now had a main role in the school play. Yes, I actually did! We were practising at lunch and most days after school. I couldn't get enough of it. I loved it. I was in my element. I actually now looked forward to school. The others in the show were nice to me also. There was a new respect for me among my peers. I was treated like I had some sort of talent. I wasn't laughed at as much anymore. This was all surreal. Is this what the past sixteen years of my life were supposed to have been like? If so, I want them back! I lost so many years through torment and unhappiness. It saddens me to think of all that time wasted.

This whole experience gave me a newfound love of life, new confidence and a new purpose. I could now wake up in the morning without fear. Social media was still an issue at times, and I was still called names by some boys. But it didn't feel the same anymore, I was not as affected as I used to be. Ever since I became good at something, or maybe ever since somebody believed in me, I seemed to have developed a harder shell, a stronger shield to defend myself against those bullies. My mindset changed and I gained respect for myself. I now looked in the mirror with less shame, less pity and more faith in what I could achieve.

Unfortunately, Mr. Jones has recently left the school; he was poached by the private schooling system. They saw his talents! I cried when I heard the news. I know it's a bit uncool to admit this, but I really miss him. I am worried about how I will cope without him around. Before he left, Mr. Jones gave a thank you card to all the students in the school play. He wrote a lovely message in mine:

'Waleed, please continue to strengthen the person inside you, the world deserves to see your amazing talents.'

This is typical of Mr. Jones, he always manages to say the right things to give me the drive to keep going, to be who I want to be, to not give up and to certainly not be the class clown anymore.

Mr. Jones used to wear a t-shirt that said 'CHOOSE LIFE'. It was to do with a band called WHAM! Yes, I've never heard of them before either! Anyway, I bought one for myself as a reminder of the positive impact Mr. Jones has had on me. I have never worn it. I have framed it in my bedroom and every day before I leave for school I look at it and tell myself… *"Waleed, choose life today."*

This will be my message for the rest of my life. Whenever I doubt myself, whenever I get bullied, whenever I feel like I don't have a purpose in life, I will look at the t-shirt in the frame and remind myself of Mr. Jones and how he made me feel. The belief he gave to me and the kindness he offered me when nobody else did. Thank you Mr. Jones, I will never forget you. I promise not to let you down, and, you know what, I also promise not to let myself down either.

Points to consider:

- Did you feel that Waleed gave up on himself too easily initially? Did he have any other choice? If so, what?

- What role did Waleed's parents play here?

- Waleed mentioned that there was no judgement present in primary school; what do you think is possible in life without judgement?

- Mr. Jones clearly had a positive impact; what did he do so well that helped Waleed?

- Is there anything that concerns you about the relationship between Waleed and Mr. Jones?

- Do you have a 'Mr. Jones' in your life?

What does the CMB Wellbeing Warrior say?

Waleed came out of this whole experience positively, right? That's what it sounds like anyway. However, if we really delve into Waleed's feelings here, I have no doubt that he would want to focus on the past and his 'lost sixteen years'. Can you remember the comment he made on this?

As he is the client, we would discuss his agenda and the topic he wants to focus on. However, to be an effective coach for Waleed, I would try and stray away from the past and focus on the here and now. As stated previously, many clients tend to drive coaching conversations down memory lane. This can be dangerous territory, and is more of an area for a psychotherapist, who would focus on the client's psychological history. Notwithstanding this, as mentioned in earlier chapters, some coaching sessions may examine past experiences. When doing this, it is important to apply it in the correct manner, where there is a forward-looking reason behind such a decision.

Coaching sessions can easily be seen as an opportunity to 'let off some steam'. Waleed could potentially find himself using this time to complain about his parents and the diet they gave him growing up, or complain about how the boys treated him at school, or even complain about the school not doing much to support his situation.

As Waleed's coach, I would not be doing him any justice just to sit there and allow him to do so. In this instance, he would not be getting full value for the time he has invested into the session. Instead, it would be beneficial to develop the cognitive skills that will support him through his challenges.

In Waleed's story, he has used the word 'purpose' a few times. Did you notice that? I see a pattern arising and I would go with that, a pattern of emptiness or lack of self-direction.

The term 'purpose' can mean different things to different people. However, your life purpose is yours, you own it.

Have you seen the film Bee Movie? For me, it demonstrates the bees' purpose perfectly. Once they lost their purpose, they themselves were lost. They needed a purpose to live and to survive. Check it out!

It sounds like Waleed was in a similar situation to the bees. We can all relate to this at times, we all need to have a purpose.

When I ask clients on the spot what their life purpose is, there is almost always a pause, a long pause. Have you ever asked yourself this question? Why am I here? What purpose do I have in this world? If you have, well done to you, you are among the few, based on the responses I have received during coaching sessions.

Waleed would be forgiven for believing that his purpose was to make others laugh. This could be due to how he sees himself, based on the influence his behaviour has on others and what people expect of him.

He actually used the term 'please others'. This can be common among those who just want to be accepted and approved in social groupings. We all have 'pleasers' in our lives; can you identify any? Are you one? If so, what are you feeling right now? Who are you pleasing? What effect is it having on you?

Waleed has essentially accepted that his role is to 'please' others, to serve them laughter and to entertain on a daily basis. It's constant and eventually takes its toll. This type of behaviour generally leads to burnout and resentment of oneself. Did you notice this happening?

When he described the scene of looking into the mirror and running out of tissues, he was clearly running on empty; at the bottom of the barrel. He had given up on himself at this stage. Whatever purpose he may have had was gone.

Waleed now needs to find a new purpose and bring it to light. Remember, we can choose how we think about something. We need to convey this to Waleed, that he can take control of his thoughts. Here, we create an appetite for Waleed to expect more from himself. To be able to look into that same mirror and like what he sees, perhaps even love what he sees! He is better than the class clown and he owes it to himself to do something about it.

Waleed has already started his journey, cohesively, we just need to guide it and make it sustainable, as there were concerns with Mr. Jones' absence.

Deciding on your life purpose takes some thought, it cannot be rushed. During a coaching session, we would unearth Waleed's life purpose, through the use of the *CMB Masterful Mission*. In this instance, I would ask Waleed to make some notes and attempt to come up with his life purpose in his own time, under his own supervision, and with no pressure from a coach involved. If this is conducted on the spot, there is an element of, "Oh, I better come up with something, so here it goes." But we cannot rush this. It needs care, deep thought and sentiment. Waleed would then bring his purpose statement to his next session, where we would discuss it further and see where in life it could be utilised.

Over the course of the coaching programme, it is common for a client's life purpose to change. This is absolutely fine and comes about as a result of people beginning to understand themselves more on a deeper level. It is an evolving practice that involves continued refining.

Waleed will eventually create a life purpose statement that he is happy with. A purpose that fills his emptiness and creates a clear message to himself about his own 'why?' and a justification for his presence on this planet. This will provide him with a solid tool to use whenever his purpose is in doubt. Try it, it really is a simple yet effective tool to use if you ever find yourself questioning your own purpose in life.

Enquiry Questions:

Clearly, Waleed's Drama teacher has left a gap in Waleed's life by moving on. This is common practice in school as students build a positive relationship with teachers, who sometimes then move on. Waleed was evidently very fond of Mr. Jones, and it sounds like he instilled great confidence in Waleed. If Waleed feels that he is falling back into old habits without Mr. Jones being in his life, what would you tell him to do? What options does Waleed have?

CMB Task:

A few tasks for this one!

Task 1: Make some time for yourself. Sit somewhere peaceful and think of what you bring to the life you are in. What are you here to do? What have you been doing so far? What really is your purpose on this planet?

Design your life purpose. Write down a life purpose statement that truly represents you. Remember this is not concrete; revisit and redesign if and when needed.

Task 2: Waleed has described himself as a 'pleaser' to others. This cannot be a nice place for him to be in. Look around you to see the behaviour of those in your circles. Who is the pleaser? Why are they behaving like this? What can you do to support them in not feeling the need to 'please' others? If you behave like this, can you coach yourself into changing this behaviour?

Task 3: Finally, take a break over the next few days. Grab your favourite drink and some popcorn and sit with a family member or friend and watch the Bee Movie. Identify the purpose of the bees and analyse what happens when their purpose disappears. Enjoy!

19

Imara: The Torment Of Being An Immigrant

My first minute, hour, day, week, month and year in a new country was not easy. Right away the odds were against me, I couldn't even speak the language properly! In the beginning, I was sleeping rough, eating what I could and simply surviving. This was tough, unexpected, but this is where ambition meets opportunity I'm told, it's gotta be better than this...right?

After some time getting sorted, and with the support of the police and local authorities, I was lucky to be accepted into a school. This was an amazing break for me and this was the beginning of my future; a bright future in a wonderful 'opportunistic' country like England.

Before I left home, I watched videos of English schools and could see how happy all the students were and the amazing facilities these schools had. Lovely uniforms, sports pitches, swimming pools and 'free' food. It all amazed me and it was a far cry from my school back home.

The particular school I ended up in seemed quite different however. The school building was very old. It looked 'tired' even, paint falling off the walls, doors hanging off hinges, and windows so loose the rain was coming in. Nonetheless, it was better than no school, right?

That's what I kept telling myself. The teachers were very helpful. Very kind. In fact, I've never experienced such kindness and support like it.

On my first day at this school, I remember sitting in silence and being completely lost. I didn't know how to communicate, in fact I couldn't communicate. A boy called Ben was assigned as my buddy for the day. He was nice. I just followed him around and did what he was doing. In hindsight, maybe I followed him too closely. He went to the toilet and had to ask me to leave, which was an awkward moment, to say the least!

People were looking at me strangely; they were staring at me, unsurprisingly, as I looked out of place. My hair was wild and long and my skin was pretty rough. I was wearing a borrowed old school uniform from the lost and found stash. It was too big for me; the blazer was literally drooping over me, and the shoes, well, they were my form tutor's old ones!

The main problem was that I looked much older than everybody else. I had facial hair above my lip. Nobody else in the year group did. I stood out like a sore thumb, so of course they were looking at me with curiosity. I probably looked like I'd escaped from prison or something! But, you know what? I did. I did escape from prison. I was a prisoner of war back home.

In my classes, I just sat there, as I didn't know what was going on. I was completely oblivious to what was being taught. The teacher was giving instructions and I didn't understand a thing. I just heard noise, words that I had never heard before. I couldn't engage and I didn't know what to do.

Break time arrived. I was approached by a boy:

"F**k you," he said.

"Huh?" I responded in a concerned and confused tone!

At the time I didn't understand him, but by the look on his face I could tell it wasn't good and I wasn't welcome. This was the pattern of my next few months. I didn't feel welcome, not one bit!

I tried to improve my English, I tried really hard. The inclusion teacher was fantastic. Ms. Pachlawski was her name. As she was Polish, I think she understood the challenges of being treated like an 'outsider', learning a new language and not being able to communicate with others effectively. Each day I had a lesson with Ms. Pachlawski. This was the happiest part of my day. I felt safe with her, she understood me, she would *listen* to me.

Unfortunately, I didn't feel safe all day in school. Break and lunchtimes were the worst. I even used to wish that school had no breaks and that we could just continue with the lessons. I simply didn't feel protected at break and lunchtimes. Yes, I had some nice people in my lessons, but once break and lunchtime came, they all played football and stuff. So at every break or lunchtime I was exposed to nasty people. I was alone; easy prey for the wolves!

> I felt safe with her, she understood me,
> she would *listen* to me.

Who would want to hang out with me anyway? I could see why they wouldn't want to. I couldn't communicate, so I was not much company. And my looks, they would put anyone off! As I said, I looked 'different', I looked older, much older! To be honest, I didn't even know my real date of birth, so I didn't know what my real age was.

I had facial hair and they didn't. I was much larger than them and, as for my voice, it was different to theirs, very different, more like a man than a boy. I probably smelt too. I got to wash once per week. Hygiene wasn't a priority for me back then; survival was! So yes, nobody wanted anything to do with me.

One of my most challenging days came about two weeks after I joined. It all started in a Maths lesson just before lunchtime. The teacher asked me a question in front of the whole class. At this stage, my English was improving, but just to a basic level. I was asked to do a sum in my head, a mental maths question. This was something I could do on paper with no problem, but in my head it was a whole new ball game. I cannot remember the actual question, but let's just say it was '20 - 5 x 12 + 27 =?' As soon as the question was asked, I immediately shut down and went into closed mode, where I simply sat and stared into space, waiting for the teacher to move onto another student. I didn't know the answer, so that was it. I didn't believe I could do it, especially under the pressure of everyone watching.

Inside I was thinking: *Please ask somebody else quickly!* But no. The teacher continued, "C'mon Imara, you can do this, right?"

But I couldn't, I didn't have the confidence.

To make it worse, he said, "I will sit here until you get it," and to make it even worse again, all the other students were now putting up their hand to answer it.

Just give me a break here sir, I thought to myself.

The pressure was on. I didn't know what to do. I sat and sat, red-faced and starting to panic. This was getting really uncomfortable.

On reflection, I wish I had the communication skills to be able to say, "Thank you sir, but I cannot answer this question, please can you either help me or ask somebody else."

Time went on and I was still sitting there, the centre of attention, completely out of my comfort zone. This was humiliating. *Why is the teacher doing this to me?* I kept asking myself.

Everyone was looking at me with either pity or joy from being entertained, at my expense! Eventually, the teacher gave in and asked somebody else to answer. This was embarrassingly bad for me and my image, but not as bad as what was coming later.

At lunchtime, I was eating alone, as always. A group of boys who had never been nice to me started looking over towards me and laughing. They began throwing food at me and shouting, "Eat immigrant, eat!" They start throwing more and more. I didn't react. Then, one boy, called Alan, walked over to me and said, "You are dumb, you can't even speak and you can't count." He then spilt water on my trousers and shouted, "Uhhhh, disgusting, the immigrant p****d himself."

I couldn't take any more. A sea of rage hit me and I lost control. BANG! I punched him. He was on the floor and couldn't move. I hit him good, hard, probably too hard. I didn't know my own strength; remember I was much bigger than him!

OK, I thought to myself, *that had to be done, I have sent a message here, he won't annoy me again.*

But then, along came his friends and they all jumped on me. I was lying on the floor and they were punching and kicking me. This was terrible. I was hurt and bleeding from my nose and mouth. Then the teacher arrived and they all ran. The teacher took me into his room and I was asked to write a statement. "A STATEMENT? I can barely write my name," I 'tried' to explain!

This was not good. I was in trouble and warned that if this happened again, I was out. I felt frustrated; this was so unfair. I was just trying to protect myself. What kind of system is this? I left the teacher's office and my lip was swollen. I had lumps in my head and my ribs hurt real bad; they were black and blue. *Land of opportunity?* I think to myself. This was a hard time for me.

Thankfully there was something positive I could take from my first year in England: PE, and cricket in particular, gave me great joy. As I have already mentioned, I was bigger and older than the rest. This had its advantages. The PE teacher, Mr. Jameson, was so good to me. He gave me sports clothes (his own I think) and he arranged for me to do additional sports outside of school. Clothes, food, transport, you name it, he covered all my expenses in order to help me.

He used sports as an opportunity for me to showcase my talent to others, where I gained credibility, acceptance and popularity. Amusingly, although he never admitted this, many times he used our PE lessons as a platform for me to get my own back on the boys in the class who were troublesome, and who in particular gave me a hard time. Some of them were OK, but others were difficult, very rude. Difficult and rude to the teachers also, with a real lack of care and respect towards them. This was a smart move from him!

For example, one day Mr. Jameson was teaching rugby and the skill of how to tackle. "Imara!" he called out, as he showed me what to do.

"Alan!" he then shouted, "Can you please do this demonstration with Imara?"

Now, Alan and I had history and, as you know, Alan was not a nice person. He had a weasel look about him, which could also describe his personality! He made life difficult, not only for me, but other students and teachers. I even saw him attack a teacher. Honestly, he was not right upstairs...

"OK," said Mr. Jameson, "Alan, you stand there and Imara, you take the ball at speed," as he physically manoeuvred us into position. "Alan, your role is to stop him."

Alan was standing there with an anxious look on his face. "But sir, but sir, this is not for me, rugby is not my thing."

Mr. Jameson then winked at me. I will never know for sure, but I think that wink was a message to me, as if to say, "Go on lad, this is your chance to show him your strength. He deserves it for what he puts you through."

As I thought this is what he meant, I went for it, if it wasn't, then... oops! BANG! I literally hit Alan as hard as I could and trampled right over him. He was flat on the floor and, to make it even better, everybody else was laughing at him.

He slowly got up, wiped himself down and pretended that he was OK, but we all knew he wasn't. He was in bits as he uncomfortably limped away.

I walked over to him and asked, "Are you OK Alan?" He reacted with a confused look on his face. He was clearly surprised that after everything he had put me through, I could still be nice to him.

I understand that you may think I should not have been nice to him because he was so unpleasant to me, however, I did this because I wanted to make friends, not enemies. Sport was an opportunity for me to connect with people. I needed to connect. School was hard. Life in general was hard for me. It was lonely. I needed to take whatever opportunity I could to support me through it. So I did. I consoled Alan in front of everybody and, thankfully, ever since then, our relationship has been so much better. My behaviour sent everybody a message, it demonstrated the type of person I was. I was proud of this. I still am.

This moment was the turning point for me. The boys in the class gained a new respect for me because I was good at sport. For many sports, I was one of the first picked. This made me happy. Cricket ended up being the best thing in my life. Mr. Jameson learned very quickly that I had a talent. I made the school squad with ease and I was always the first up to bat. In each game I scored many runs and won every match for the team single-handedly. This is not me being arrogant, just truthful; the stats don't lie!

OK, I confess, as previously stated, I was bigger and probably older than the other players, so maybe I had an advantage, just maybe…!

It was funny actually. Every match we played, the boys from the other school would ask me my age, and my teammates would just laugh. Even the opposing teacher would sometimes comment on me. Mr. Jameson would just smile, as if to say, "Yes, he probably is older, but according to the papers, he is underage." These were happy times. Sport brought the best out of all of us.

Thankfully, today I'm still playing cricket and building relationships with more people. This improves my speaking skills and my confidence. I have been selected for the county cricket squads and things are looking up.

Has the move been a success for me? Yes, it has. The challenges I faced on arrival were extremely difficult, but I will use this experience to make me stronger. I believe I can have a real impact in this country. I just need people to not treat me like an outsider and to be given a fair chance. If this happens, I will take every opportunity that comes my way.

Points to consider:

- What part of this story do you think was the most challenging for Imara? Arriving in a new country? Alan the bully? The difficulty of communicating with people? The embarrassing situation in Maths class? Looking different, or possibly his clothes and hygiene problems?

- How do you think Imara felt when he realised that his perception of English schools was very different to the one he is attending?

- Is there anything Imara's Maths teacher could have done to save Imara from the embarrassing situation he found himself in?

- What could Imara have done to protect himself during school breaks?

- How did you feel when Imara got in trouble for fighting?

- What can we learn from Imara on how he conducted himself with Alan during PE?

What does the CMB Wellbeing Warrior say?

Like every story, there are many areas to acknowledge, and I have never met a client where they finished a coaching programme and just discussed one topic. Everything is connected and, once the mind of a client is unravelled, we unearth a whole new world of thoughts and fears that potentially stop them from being fully true to themselves.

Imara has come a long way and clearly possesses a great deal of resilience and commitment to wanting a better life. However, you can sense his loneliness, as he tells his story and the torment he has experienced. Through his expression when speaking about Ms. Pachlawski and how safe he feels, we immediately see one of his values.

A 'value' is something that we believe in, that is personally important to us. It can be very helpful to know your values, as it promotes self-awareness and provides you with a guide of what is meaningful to you. In this instance, we could conduct a session on values with Imara, and through the *CMB Amicable Value Adventure*, he would complete an activity on a series of visualisations to reveal what he values in life. After this initial assessment, the next step is to see which values he is currently honouring. This will identify the values that he may be neglecting and therefore determine what areas need more exploration for future application in his life.

Let's now analyse Imara's behaviour in the canteen, where he expressed that he lost control. Do you understand why he lost control? Can you empathise with him? Do you think that he was pushed to the limit and had no other option? Was he wrong to react?

In a coaching session, I refer to this as a person's *'Raging Rhino'*. We all have one. Just like what happened to Imara, this comes alive when we are pushed to a limit and simply lose it. It is when the emotions of the situation become overwhelming and we feel that the only way out is to demonstrate aggressive behaviour. What's your limit until your *'Raging Rhino'* enters the room?

It is critical here that we examine Imara's *'Raging Rhino'* and figure out what triggers it. It is clear from the story that fighting the boys was not helpful, as his school place could be in jeopardy because of this behaviour. Once we know the trigger, we can then attempt to keep our distance, or bypass certain things that make us lose control through anger. What do you think Imara's trigger was?

In addition, we can learn to 'tame' our 'Raging Rhino'. What I mean by this is to 'soften' it, where it is less impactful. To achieve this, we need to learn how to handle this side of our personality and discover new ways of how to behave in certain situations.

I am sure you will agree that we don't always function the same way every day. Have you ever used the term 'I'm not myself today'? This demonstrates that we believe we have more than one type of personality within us. We have good and bad days, where sometimes we perform better than others. It is important to examine that, if your approach or behaviour to each day was different, what would the outcome be? Who are you 'being' when it's a good day and vice versa?

Regarding the type of behaviour that brings to light your 'Raging Rhino', we need to consider how we manage the aggressive part of this personality and develop the skills to respond, as opposed to react, when faced with a challenge. How many of us have left an argument and thought, *Ah, I wish I had said that, or, I should have done this?* We all have, it's very common. Responding, as opposed to reacting, is critical in order to achieve the desired outcome.

Changing behaviour is not easy and takes time. During a coaching session to support this, I introduce the 'Wise Wizard' again. Do you remember this? Here, we discuss when you experienced a challenging situation and your response was appropriate and successful. We go through a series of examples and investigate your successful behavioural traits when dealing with altercations.

Eventually, a client will create the personality traits for their own 'Wise Wizard'. The next step here is to make the 'Wise Wizard' more powerful than the 'Raging Rhino', by learning how to divert the behaviour that comes with it. This is achieved when a person can redirect the energy from the *'Raging Rhino'* to the *'Wise Wizard'*, and therefore make better behavioural choices. This doesn't come easy, the battle is now on between them both!

I do appreciate that these character names may sound a bit strange, but trust me, by simplifying them like this, they can be remembered easily and applied effectively.

Enquiry Questions:

Do you know somebody who is new to your country? How has your behaviour been towards them? Think of how they would describe your behaviour when you engaged with them. Is there anything you could have done differently to make them feel more welcome?

Imara's *'Raging Rhino'* was ignited because the boys continued to throw food at him and poured water over him. When was the last time your *'Raging Rhino'* came alive? What was the trigger? What was the consequence of allowing it to take control? And on reflection, what could you have done differently?

CMB Task:

What are your values? Write a list of what you value in life, selecting at least five. For example, family, friendships, health, recreation or education. Give them a score out of ten on how much you are currently honouring them. Look at the ones that are on the lower end of the scale. What can you do to honour them more?

20

Amelia: My Abusive Parents

Hello, I'm Amelia. This is the first time I have ever spoken about this openly. My hands are literally shaking here right now, but I want to do this, I want to tell my story. Thank you for hearing me out.

It all started when I was very young, as young as five actually. For as long as I can remember, it was clear that I lived in a disjointed household. My mum was never around, and my dad, well, you will hear all about him soon. I'll give you a picture of how it was. We lived in a normal three-bedroomed house on a housing estate. It was fine when compared to many others I know. Both my parents worked, so money was never a major issue, but we were certainly not rich!

My parents had an arranged marriage. I was the firstborn, and then my sister and brother came afterwards. I am very close to my siblings, I love them dearly. I do everything for them, but this is the root of many problems for me. As my mum and dad were never around, I was left with my younger siblings most of the time. I was given the role of a 'mum' way too early in my own life. I had to grow up fast, too fast in fact. My parents stole my childhood away from me, they really did. I'll never get that time back, this upsets me very much, even to this day.

Mum was much younger than dad. She was attractive and liked to look after herself, she was quite the socialite! She had a group of girlfriends that she would hang out with, all her age, but unmarried. She was living quite a party lifestyle. This brought many problems. Just before leaving the house for her 'daily gathering' with friends, dad would question what she was wearing: "You are not leaving the house looking like that," or "Who are you trying to impress?" and the most common one, "Do you not have any respect for me?"

To be perfectly honest, at this stage I was on dad's side. Clearly, he was right, she didn't have any respect for him. I mean, what kind of wife goes out socialising most nights dressed like a 19-year-old? We all knew what was going on. She was always protective of her phone and I sometimes saw other people drop her off home around the corner of the house after a night out.

Things soon got worse. People at school began to talk. Word on the street had it that she was attracting the wrong kind of attention. It was as if she was getting a name for herself, and not such a pleasant name. This was difficult for me, to say the least!

In her defence, she got married very young and didn't have a say in the matter. The decision was taken out of her hands, something I'm eager to be in control of myself. She told me the stories about her own ambitions and how she had a vision of her dream husband and family life. My grandparents clearly didn't *listen* to her, as they forced her into the life she clearly resents.

This vision was evidently a far cry from where she is now. Let's be frank, dad certainly was not her 'Prince Charming'. Still, this was no excuse for the way she behaved. Any man deserved better than that, and so did we, her children. We deserved a mother who would be there for us. A mother who did what most mothers do, and simply cared for her children. Was this too much to expect?

In reality, it was her absence that exposed me to the monster, the monster inside my dad!

I didn't really get to know dad in a normal father/daughter way. He was distant and always out working, well, at least I thought he was. He would leave the house early in the morning and return late at night. It was rare for an overlap, where both mum and dad were in the house together. When there was an overlap, it wasn't good.

> My grandparents clearly didn't *listen* to her,
> as they forced her into the life she clearly resents.

Dad knew what mum was up to. We all did, it was as clear as day to everyone, yes EVERYONE! I still remember the arguments, constant arguments and sometimes physical aggression from both of them towards each other. Clearly, there was no love in this marriage anymore. Maybe there never was! Too often the threat of divorce came up, and to be honest I used to wish that they would just go and do it. Living among them was torturous. It wasn't healthy for any of us. What chance in life did my siblings and I have? I was ashamed of my parents.

Alcohol played a large role. It seemed to get worse and worse as I got older. Maybe it was always there, I just didn't see it when I was younger. Dad would come home drunk and mum would leave after she finished off her daily bottle of wine. She would then return in the early hours of the morning and sleep on the sofa.

It was in these hours during mum's recreational lifestyle that the abuse from dad started. At first, it was verbal. He would make comments to me, insulting comments: "Stop behaving like your mother," "You do as I say," "You all think you are better than me," and so on.

Then one day he grabbed me and shoved me into the wall. I smashed my head. OK, I had answered him back, I 'forgot my place' as he put it. Still, this was frightening. To this day, I can still see his devil eyes when I think back to this moment. He looked like a man possessed, animal-like behaviour, fuelled with anger and rage. He was dangerous.

It only got worse from there. I won't go into all the details, but let's just say I was left with bruises many times. I told mum and she said she had my back, but to what extent? She still left me at home with him most nights, so did she really have my back? She prioritised her social life over her child's safety. Try to figure that one out!

I ran out of the house a few times. I needed out. I felt that I couldn't last any longer. I don't mean I was considering suicide or anything, this was never an option. I could not do that to my brother and sister as they needed me. I needed to protect them from that monster. If he was capable of what he did to me, I could only imagine what else he could end up doing.

The abuse affected me greatly. I was turning up to school in no fit state to learn. I had to wear thick layers of makeup just to cover up the marks on my face and body. My uniform stunk of cigarette smoke and I never had my homework done, because I simply didn't have the time to do it while making my siblings dinner, washing them, and eventually trying to hide from my drunk abusive father! What hope did I have in education?

My school was very supportive when I approached them with my problems. I had to, something needed to change. I was getting bad grades and ending up in detention for not completing homework. I had a lovely form tutor and Head of Year. They were always there for me. From arranging counselling to engaging with the police when things at home escalated, my school had my back. In fact, I'm not sure if I would have made it without such wonderful people sheltering me and caring for me.

The abuse from dad resulted in me having internal anger. It changed me. It ignited a rage within me. It created feelings of us (my siblings and I) against the world, a separation from our parents.

Eventually, I was sent to a specialist doctor. She was using terms such as depression and anxiety. I didn't pay much attention to this, as I hear these words from my parents all the time. I simply didn't want to know, so I blocked her advice out. I was not going down that path.

My school organised an extracurricular activity of self-defence classes, and I saw this as an opportunity. It was time to not only defend myself, but also to fight back. The first line of defence is attack, right? After only a few classes I learned skills that provided me with the tools to show my dad that it was not all on his terms anymore.

One particular assault unearthed something inside of me. I literally couldn't recognise myself. I was like an animal now. Let's just say dad got a taste of his own medicine! He now knew that things were about to change. I wouldn't be walked over any longer!

It was fulfilling and rewarding that I could apply my new skills, but also worrying, to an extent, as there was now a destructive part of my personality present. *Nobody will ever hurt me again, I'll make sure of it.* That was my new attitude. A new me was born. What has he created?

Although dad now got the message, on reflection, this part of my personality didn't do much to serve me outside the house. It was taking over from who I was. I found myself getting into altercations at school and then, BOOM, this anger within me came alive. When I was like this, it was scary and dangerous. Defensive thoughts stuck in my mind, which was lethal because it became uncontrollable. *"How dare you think you can treat me like that?"* was a daily phrase I would use. People were afraid of me, I became intimidating to others. This wasn't a good place to be in. Where has Amelia gone?

It was like dad had passed his own monster onto me. This type of behaviour got me into all sorts of trouble. I was now the one abusing others. I inflicted pain on many people who stood in my way. I just couldn't walk away from controversy; there was now a beast within me and it seized every opportunity to come out. Any sign of danger and 'it' reacted.

The abuse from dad clearly had an impact on my personality. Yes, I knew how to stand up and fend for myself, but at what cost?

The teachers who supported me all along at school were still there for me, but it was different. I could feel it. I could sense their disappointment in me. I completely got it. I was being abused and they supported me, but now I was the abuser. The roles were reversed, yet they still felt the need to support me.

I hate who I am now and don't want to behave like this. I want to change. I'm not welcoming or approachable to others, I get it. I'm not fun and I have a tendency to lose it, so who would want to be my friend? I've been called all sorts, from 'Wacko' and 'Weirdo' to 'Crazy' and 'Creep' and, because of this, creating and maintaining friendships is challenging.

My upbringing was dominated by our home life problems, and I never had the chance to build relationships with people of my own age group. I just didn't have the skillset, as I never got exposed to developing it. There was simply minimal engagement with others outside the home due to our in-house challenges. I'm still very cautious about who I let in and who I trust, so I suppose you can say I'm pretty much a loner now. Not being wanted by others, together with me being selective, probably isn't a good combination for building friendships.

This is where I am today with friends. I don't have many people to turn to. The other day, I looked in the mirror and simply saw emptiness. The reflection in the mirror was not me. I could see a tired, abused and bewildered young woman, longing for this monster to get out of her in order to be a better, more welcoming person. I asked myself the questions, *Who are you now Amelia? Have you turned into your dad?*

Points to consider:

- How do you feel about Amelia here? Is she a good person or a bad person, or something in between?

- If she is the monster now, is it her fault?

- Assuming that you have a one-dimensional opinion here, how could you challenge it?

- Using the skills you have learned throughout this book, could you try and understand her parents' perspective?

- Mum deserves her dream family life, right? Doesn't dad deserve to be respected?

- What about Amelia and her siblings: don't they deserve to be safe?

- Play devil's advocate for all parties involved and see where you end up.

What does the CMB Wellbeing Warrior say?

After playing around with each possible perspective, there are still things that need addressing. It is clear that there is a major element of neglect present in this story. Neglect from both parents. Then we have the abuse. This is extremely distressing, and I would communicate such concerns to the relevant organisations in this case.

We could discuss fairness and blame all day, but this will not serve Amelia in moving forwards. The key here is to address who Amelia is now and who she wants to be. Her identity is clearly causing her some confusion. She has distinctly expressed that she doesn't want to be this angry, uncontrollable person. This alone is positive news, as it means that she wants to change. In any coaching conversation, this is a key factor towards success.

As a coach, you can only do so much. Essentially the client needs to want to change. It cannot be forced and has to come from within, albeit with support, motivation and skills that can make change achievable. Inevitably, it is the client that maximises their own resources in order to make the transformation happen.

Change is not always easy, but it can be realised very simply by utilising resources that are already available. Through the *CMB Performance Character Creator*, we examine Amelia's character strengths. Character strengths are defined by Professor CP Niemiec as positive, trait-like capacities for thinking, feeling and behaving in ways that benefit oneself and others. As previously stated, it is recommended to keep coaching in the present and future. However as also highlighted, in some cases we create an exception, and one worth creating due to the powerful impact it can have.

This activity is similar to that of the *'Inner leader'*, as demonstrated in Chapter 11 with Marco, only this time through the use of the 'character' presented on a particular challenge.

To achieve this, we would conduct a number of exercises, wherein I would ask Amelia to reflect on past challenging experiences and relive them and her whole experience in great depth. During this emotional yet effective process, we look at the outcome and identify the character presented that contributed to the specific outcome.

Essentially, Amelia would see who she is 'being' in certain situations and begin to separate behaviours into positive and negative outcomes. She would then focus on those that demonstrate success and fulfilment and unveil a range of character strengths that she can call upon when needing support to overcome a new challenge. For example, if 'courage' was highlighted to support a particular situation, then Amelia simply needs to apply more of this in her life. Once an awareness is in place of what character strengths serve her, she is then in a good position to deal with whatever is placed in front of her. Ideally, we want to remind Amelia of who she is at her best, the artillery she has at her disposal, and who she needs to be in certain environments.

Amelia highlighted the creation of her own monster or animal-like behaviour. As previously stated in Imara's story, we can all tend to lose it. Can you remember how I would tackle this type of behaviour during a coaching session?

We would discuss the *'Raging Rhino'*. We would explore the behaviours, the triggers and the destruction that results, and examine how to take control of them by taming her *'Raging Rhino'*.

Enquiry Questions:

When reflecting back on Amelia's story, from her challenges, what character strengths do you think she demonstrated? If unsure, research them and see what you come up with. In order to get a good feel of this, attempt to think deeply and really visualise what Amelia has experienced. Because of her demanding upbringing, there is certainly a lot to work with here!

Amelia took control by communicating her feelings with the relevant people in her school. They provided some badly needed support. Think of a challenging situation you may find yourself in. Who in your network can support you with this?

CMB Task:

Take a good look at yourself. What do you see? Look deep into your character strengths. Reflect on times where you felt challenged and identify the behaviours that you used to break through such challenges. Repeat this across different challenging situations and make a list of the character traits that resulted in a positive outcome. This can support you in designing your own character strengths. Now identify where in life you can apply such traits.

Conclusion

What a journey we have been on with these wonderful students. I have no doubt that you experienced a range of emotions throughout, I certainly did. It was such a pleasure to be able to give these students a voice. A voice that many of us can relate to.

The coaching skills that you have learned within this book are by no means the answers to all your problems, however, they are a tool that can be applied alongside other resources.

Thank you for taking the time to read this book. It is something I am very proud to be part of, and I sincerely hope it will support you in your own personal journey. With the vast amount of skills disclosed, I understand that some things may be forgotten. However, the key message is to *listen*: *listen* to the people around you, and *listen* to yourself. Remember to take control of your life, maximise your resources, explore your options, don't be afraid to make mistakes, act upon what needs to be done and simply go and do it. If this doesn't work for you, repeat using a different approach.

Through these stories, we witnessed on many occasions a call for help from the storyteller. The word *listen* was used in each one. Please explore the *CMB Enquiry Questions* and *CMB Tasks* and see how you can support yourself and others around you to listen.

Remember, the people in your life cannot listen unless you tell them that there is a problem. Your own voice is a great resource, so please use it to support you. Don't be afraid to ask for help and speak out whenever needed. You really can make a difference, by openly communicating and working positively together with your family, teachers and friends, for example.

It is clear from the stories how unpleasant people can be towards each other. Please think about the words you use and how you make others feel. As we have experienced, name-calling can have a lasting effect!

Finally, be proud of who you are and what you can achieve. Be kind and present when others need you and always demonstrate the best you, in whatever environment you find yourself in. It is your time. This is you!

"BE YOU, BE THE BEST YOU"

'Go raibh maith agat'

Thank you
Ciarán

Author's Bio

Ciarán McBreen is the Managing Director of CMB Coaching and Training. He is a professional mindset coach and educator who has created a platform for thousands of children and adults to flourish, develop self-belief, feel empowered and reach their true potential. Ciarán has sparked the 'life' into the lives of many.

Ciarán's passion for education and supporting others stems from his challenges as a school student. Having struggled himself in the classroom and admittedly leaving school with disappointing results, Ciarán is fully aware of the difficulties children face in education.

Now, with the credentials of an MA in Education (Coaching and Mentoring), a BA in Sports Science, a PGCE in Physical Education and a professional coaching certificate accredited by the International Coaching Federation, Ciarán has the capacity to make a positive difference to individuals of all ages and organisations within any industry.

Ciarán has put his teaching and coaching skills to practice and created the *CMB Wellbeing Warrior* programme. To date, this programme has not only improved the behaviour and lifestyles of participants, but it has also provided them with skills that support individuals for continued lifelong development.

You can find out more about Ciarán and all of the CMB Coaching and Training programmes on the following website: www.cmbcoachingandtraining.com or via his social media platforms on @cmbcoachmcbreen.

Ciarán is from Cootehill, Co. Cavan in Ireland. He is currently living in Dubai with his wife Kim, daughter Sofia, and son Harry.

Listen! 2

If you would be interested in telling your story for a sequel to LISTEN!, please scan the barcode and complete the questionnaire. Your voice deserves to be heard!

Organisations For Further Support

If you have experienced any of the challenges highlighted in LISTEN! and need further support, please refer to the below organisations:

Childline: www.childline.org.uk

NSPCC: www.nspcc.org.uk

Samaritans: www.samaritans.org

Barnardos: www.barnardos.ie

ISPCC: www.ispcc.ie

Young Minds: www.youngminds.org.uk

Mentally Healthy Schools: mentallyhealthyschools.org.uk

The Anna Freud Centre: annafreud.org

Educational support services: www.educationsupport.org.uk (A free helpline for teaching staff)

Mind: www.mind.org.uk (For adults needing support)

LIFT Ireland: www.liftireland.ie

Social Media

Feel free to follow me on social media and share your thoughts on my book and each specific story. Your engagement is very welcome, and, you never know, the student behind the story may see it. You could make their day!

Instagram: www.instagram.com/cmbcoachmcbreen

Facebook: www.facebook.com/cmbcoachmcbreen

Twitter: www.twitter.com/cmbcoachmcbreen

Youtube: www.youtube.com/channel/CMBCoachMcBreen

LinkedIn: www.linkedin.com/in/cmbcoachmcbreen

Website: www.cmbcoachingandtraining.com

Email: info@cmbcoachingandtraining.com

PLEASE FOLLOW ME

References / Suggested Reading

Achor, S., 2010. *The happiness advantage: How a positive brain fuels success in work and life.* Currency.

Alter, A., 2017. *Irresistible: The rise of addictive technology and the business of keeping us hooked.* Penguin.

Blakemore, S.J., 2018. *Inventing ourselves: The secret life of the teenage brain.* Public Affairs.

Bonnar, L., 2019. Press Play. A Teenagers Guide to Living an Awesome Life.

Byrne, R., 2008. *The Secret.* Simon and Schuster.

Byrne, R., 2012. *The Magic.* Simon and Schuster.

Chamine, S., 2012. *Positive intelligence: Why only 20% of teams and individuals achieve their true potential and how you can achieve yours.* Greenleaf Book Group.

Clear, J., 2018. *Atomic Habits: The life-changing million copy bestseller.* Random House.

Clear, J., 2018. *Atomic Habits: Tiny changes, remarkable results: An easy & proven way to build good habits & break bad ones.* Avery.

Deci, Edward L., and Richard M. Ryan. "Self-determination theory." (2012).

Doran, J., *Ways to Well-being*

Doyle, G., 2020. *Untamed.* Dial Press.

Duckworth, A. and Duckworth, A., 2016. *Grit: The power of passion and perseverance* (Vol. 234). New York, NY: Scribner.

Dweck, C., 2017. *Mindset-updated edition: Changing the way you think to fulfil your potential.* Hachette UK.

Greenfield, S., 2002. *The private life of the brain.* Penguin UK.

Haldane, D., 2015. The Chimp Paradox.

Kolb, D.A., 2014. *Experiential learning: Experience as the source of learning and development.* FT press.

National Health Service, 2021. Grief after bereavement or loss. Available at: https://www.nhs.uk/mental-health/feelings-symptoms-behaviours/feelings-and-symptoms/grief-bereavement-loss/ (Accessed: 2/02/2021).

Robbins, T., 2007. *Awaken the giant within: How to take immediate control of your mental, emotional, physical and financial.* Simon and Schuster.

Seligman, M.E., 2012. *Flourish: A visionary new understanding of happiness and well-being.* Simon and Schuster.

Siegel, D.J., 2015. *Brainstorm: The power and purpose of the teenage brain.* Penguin.

Tolle, E., 2009. *A New Earth: create a better life.* Penguin UK

Whitmore, J., 1996. Coaching for performance. N. Brealey Pub.

Williams, M. and Penman, D., 2011. *Mindfulness: An eight-week plan for finding peace in a frantic world.* Rodale.

Printed in Great Britain
by Amazon